ALLEGANY COUNTY AREA FOUNDATION

proudly presents:

Allegany County

In the 20th Century: Stories of Change

The Allegany County Area Foundation has served the people and agencies of Allegany County since 1983 with plans of doing so when the county celebrates its three hundredth anniversary and beyond. This community foundation exists to invest the generous gifts of donors perpetually, using the growth of these funds to help scholars attend institutions of higher education and to support organizations whose projects seek to improve the quality of life for Allegany County residents.

Pooling the resources of many to do more, the Allegany Fund is unrestricted, allowing the board to make grants available to groups with a special project in mind, such as the book you are holding. Several other funds are designated to provide annual gifts to libraries, not-for-profit groups or whatever organization the donor chose. Large endowments earmarked for scholarships have provided thousands of dollars to hundreds of students as they take the first steps toward promising careers.

A popular annual event has been the Educator of the Year banquet, which honors teachers for outstanding work they do. Recognizing faculty members who have been nominated as representatives of their schools has been a positive, "good news" program which the Foundation has been proud to sponsor. Dozens of scholarships announced at the banquet illustrate the success stories teachers write every day. Teachers leaving the banquet report their pride in their chosen profession, and others mention their appreciation of the schools of Allegany County today and their optimism for the future.

As this book goes to print, the Allegany County Area Foundation address is P.O. Box 494, Wellsville, NY 14895. Its director of development is Robert P. Christian, its executive assistant is Patricia Oliver, its president is Leslie Haggstrom, and Kenneth L. Nielsen is president emeritus. Mr. Nielsen along with Leslie Haggstrom, Peter R. Sprague, Allen Schintzius, and James Searle are remembered as the organization's founders.

Other board members are Thomas P. Brown, John M. Carter, Dr. Daniel Acton, Pauletta Copenhaver, Richard Halberg, Carolyn J. Miller, Marcia Moore, Robert M. Mountain, and Patricia Regan. The generations to come will make changes, but with the support of all those who appreciate Allegany County and its residents, the future dreamed of by the founding members of a community foundation for the ages will continue.

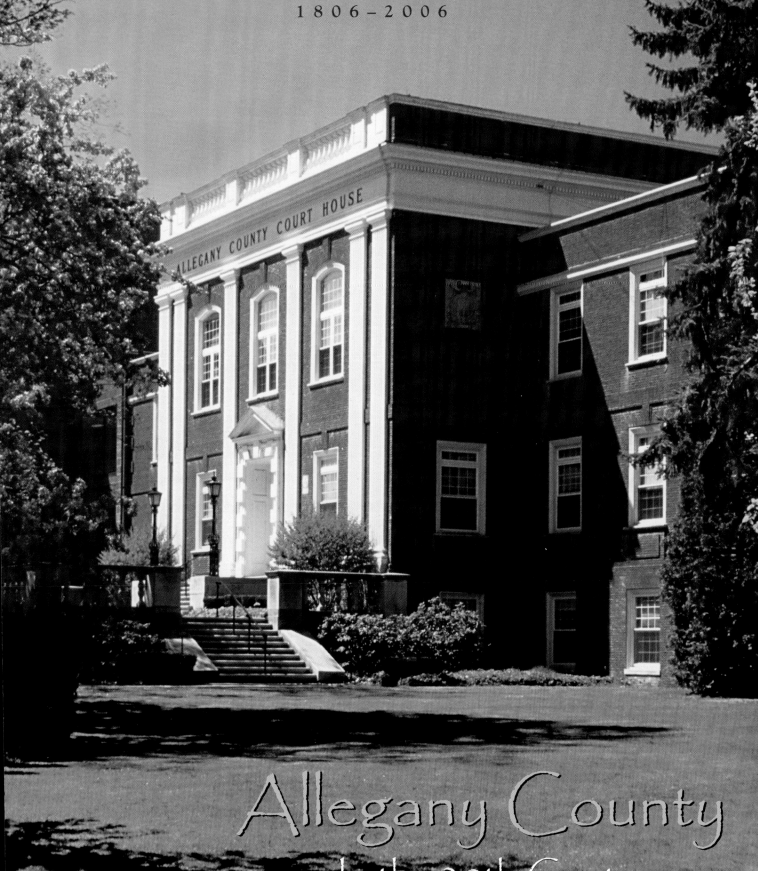

Allegany County

In the 20th Century:
Stories of Change

Table of Contents

THE
DONNING COMPANY
PUBLISHERS

The Donning Company Publishers
184 Business Park Drive, Suite 206
Virginia Beach, VA 23462

Steve Mull, General Manager
Barbara B. Buchanan, Office Manager
Richard A. Horwege, Senior Editor
Amanda D. Guilmain, Graphic Designer
Amy Thomann, Imaging Artist
Mary Ellen Wheeler, Proofreader
Susan Adams, Project Research Coordinator
Scott Rule, Director of Marketing
Stephanie Linneman, Marketing Coordinator

Mary Taylor, Project Director

Library of Congress Cataloging-in-Publication Data

Braack, Craig R.
    Allegany County in the twentieth century : stories of change / by Craig R. Braack and the Allegany County Bi-Centennial History Book Committee.
        p.   cm.
    ISBN-13: 978-1-57864-334-9 (hard cover : alk. paper)
    ISBN-10: 1-57864-334-1 (hard cover : alk. paper)
1. Allegany County (N.Y.)—History. 2. Allegany County (N.Y.)—Pictorial works. 3. Allegany County (N.Y.)—Economic conditions. 4. Business enterprises—New York (State)—Allegany County. I. Allegany County Bi-Centennial History Book Committee (Allegany, N.Y.) II. Title.
    F127.A4B73 2005
    974.7'84043—dc22   2005029788

Printed in the USA at Walsworth Publishing Company

Moss Lake

Acknowledgments

The idea for this book was conceived in 2003. We knew the journey would be long and sometimes arduous but our destination had a purpose: to document important elements of our county's twentieth century and its myriad changes. On this journey, we have encountered many wonderful people, eager to share their memories and contributions to the life and history of Allegany County. Now that our journey has ended, it is imperative to recognize the key people who helped create this book. The inherent danger is omitting some significant contributors. To these people, I offer my apologies.

Book Committee members (left to right, clockwise) are Edith Wallace, Greta Gram, Bette Stockman, Doug Clarke, Craig Braack, and Lee Gridley.

To Lee Gridley of Wellsville: Co-Editor whose enthusiasm, local historical knowledge and grammatical skills played a key role in the production of the book; these contributions are duly noted with my heartfelt appreciation.

To Bette Stockman of Friendship, note taker "extraordinaire": The book would not have evolved without your help with compiling information and preparing it for printing.

To Greta Gram and Edith Wallace both of Andover: Thanks for your research, knowledge, loyalty and humor so capably rendered for this book.

To Doug Clarke of Alfred: Thanks for your technical expertise in our amazing world of computers and digital photography.

To the Allegany County Board of Legislators and Information Technology Department: Members Deb Button, Keith Hooker, Darby Lavery, and Mike Yudichak for their continuous support and tremendous technical knowledge so capably provided with each request for help, I offer my thanks.

To the Book Committee, listed alphabetically by township, my sincere gratitude for contributing the vast majority of topics in the book:

Alfred—Galen Brooks, Mary Lou Cartledge, Doug Clarke, Jean Lang, Lyle Palmiter, Wally Higgins
Alma—Norman Ives
Almond—Lee and Donna Ryan
Andover—Robert Baker, Greta Gram, William Greene, Edith Wallace
Bolivar—Rosemary Feenaughty, Barbara Webb
Caneadea—Gertrude Hall
Centerville—Dorothy Campbell, Deborah Covert
Cuba—David Crowley, Mary Nease
Friendship—Boni Bliss, Norma Pizza, Kathleen Schumann, Pat Scott, Bette Stockman

Genesee—Jean Milliman
Grove—Marilyn Weidman
Hume—Rondus Miller
Independence—Roger Easton
Rushford—Homer Norton
Scio—Carolyn Miller, Cheryl Smith
Ward—Rose Maine
Wellsville—Diane Converso, Shirley Engle, Lee Gridley, Jane Pinney, Jean Richmond
Willing—Christina Wightman
Wirt—Betty Bartoo

In the 1930s when Franklin D. Roosevelt was governor, he persuaded the NYS Legislature to pass a bill requiring municipalities in the state to appoint a historian to acquire, preserve, and display items of local historical interest. Over the intervening years our county has been fortunate to have many fine historians serving their townships. The following town historians are serving their communities in 2005:

Alfred—Jean Lang
Allen—Patricia A. Hopkins
Alma—Ron Taylor
Almond—Almond Historical Society
Amity—Temporarily vacant
Andover—Robert Baker
Angelica—Temporarily vacant
Belfast—Paul Curcio
Birdsall—Faye Clancy
Bolivar—Rosemary Feenaughty
Burns—Sherri Reed
Caneadea—Gertrude Hall
Centerville—Deborah Covert
Clarksville—Sharon Robinson
Cuba—David Crowley

Friendship—Norma Pizza
Genesee—Jean Milliman
Granger—Loreen Bentley
Grove—Marilyn Weidman
Hume—Rondus Miller
Independence—Roger Easton
New Hudson—Temporarily vacant
Rushford—Homer Norton and Luanne Bump
Scio—Cheryl Smith
Ward—Rose Maine
Wellsville—Diane Converso
West Almond—Sharon Gadacz
Willing—Christina Wightman
Wirt—Betty Bartoo

Many others have generously contributed material and without their help, the book would not have been printed. They are listed by town:

Albany—John Scherer-NYS Museum
Angelica—Kier Dirlam, Paul Gallman, Dana Guinnip, Bill Hart, Larry Short
Avoca—John Muchler
Belfast—Rob Abraham, Wendell Chamberlain, Bill Heaney
Belmont—Diane Baker, John Foels, Jacquelyn Manis, Tom Parmenter, Larry Scholes, Scott Spillane, Randy Swarthout, John Tucker, Brenda Witter, Dave Zlomek
Buffalo—Erland Kailbourne
Bolivar—Ruby Allen
Caneadea—Dean Liddick
Canisteo—Sue and John Babbitt
Castile—Brian Scriven
Centerville—Bill Reddy
Cuba—Jeff Bradley, Dawn Santangelo
Friendship—Ronna Jordan, Tim Timbrook (NYS-DOT), Ford Easton

Hume—Ken and Jean Irwin, Dave and Trudy Schwert
Rushford—Luanne Bump, Donna and Conrad Bruckert, Lee Cobb, Rita Hunt, Rhonda Kozlowski
Rochester—Charles P. Woolever
Scio—Guy James, Kevin Kailbourne, Gloria Miess, Patience Reagan, Cathleen Whitfield
Ward—Fred Sinclair, Charles Deichmann
Wellsville—Rod Biehler, Jesse Case, Kelly Dickerson, Gretchen Fortner, Marty Fuller, Rita Gooch, Ralph and Jerry Hills, Betty Joyce, Joyce Krupnik, Sylvia Masin, Nancy Mosher, Tom O'Grady, Bob Piscitelli, Dan Russo, Bob Sanders, Bob Sobeck, Jim Stein, Art Van Tyne, Marge Vossler, Bob Weigand
Willing—David Roeske

ALLEGANY COUNTY BOARD OF LEGISLATORS

COUNTY OFFICE BUILDING * 7 COURT STREET
BELMONT, NEW YORK 14813-1083
TELEPHONE 585-268-9222 * FAX 585-268-9446

James G. Palmer
Chairman

Brenda Rigby Riehle
Clerk

April 11, 2005

As we pause to look back on the rich two-hundred year history of Allegany County, it's difficult for us to relate to how the early settlers struggled to make a life for themselves and their families in this new territory. We owe much to their vision and persistence in seeing the beauty and promise of this wonderful area.

We need to continue the efforts of these pioneers in moving our County forward into the next stages of its existence. Despite the difficulties we face, it will be well worth our efforts as we meet the many challenges of our current situation to leave a better place for the next generations.

It is my privilege, as the fourth generation of my family to live in these foothills of the Alleghenies, to serve as chairman of the Board of Legislators. As you read and enjoy the efforts of so many of our citizens to compile a snapshot of our history, I hope you will come to appreciate the rich and distinguished heritage we all share.

James G. Palmer, Chairman
Allegany County Board of Legislators

Introduction

In the long, rich history of Allegany County, many yesterdays have come and gone, many tomorrows will come and go. What happened in between was the primary focus of this book. Our goal was to effectively cover the concept of change in our county during the twentieth century. We further felt it was

mandatory to "pay our historic respects" to the previous countywide published history books: Beers Company's 1879 *History of Allegany County* and County Historian John Stearns Minard's 1895 *Allegany County and Its People: A Centennial Memorial History of Allegany County, New York*. This book marked the centennial celebration of the first permanent settler, Nathaniel Dyke, who moved into the Elm Valley area in 1795. It is theorized the Beers Company published many different county books as a result of local historical interest generated by the nation's Centennial of 1876 in Philadelphia.

Umbrellas kept the sun off of several attendees at the Allegany County Centennial Celebration held at Elm Valley in 1895.

The New York State Senate passed a bill on March 7,1806, authorizing the creation of Allegany County. A similar bill was passed in the New York State Assembly on April 4, 1806. A Council of Revision approved their actions and our county became a legal entity on April 7, 1806. We were the first county to be formed from Genesee County which had comprised all of present-day Western New York.

The twentieth century has seen the most rapid changes in the history of mankind. In 1900, roads were unpaved and "rapid" communication was only by telephone, then in its infancy. The last hundred years have seen our roads paved and develop into quality networks to facilitate travel in comfort. Primitive telephone service has developed into networking with computers giving us instant, quality and dependable communications around the world.

While numerous comprehensive historical publications have been produced for village/town centennial and/or sesquicentennial anniversaries, there has not been a countywide history publication covering the twentieth century. Our book committee debated long and hard over what topics, events, and subjects to include. The final decision includes topics that represent the inevitable element of change and how they affected the county as a whole or a large portion thereof. Perhaps umbrage will be taken over topics or places not included, specifically churches and businesses, as they are too numerous for the scope of this book. For these people I have empathy. We simply couldn't write about everything of importance to all people.

Respectfully,
Craig R. Braack, County Historian, Book Editor

chapter

HISTORY UPDATED

Our ever-growing knowledge in science and technology combined with the element of time have granted us new opportunities for garnering additional information and re-evaluating previously published accounts of seventeenth to nineteenth century events in our county. We would be remiss if we did not address some of these "new" discoveries that now shed fresh light on our past. By these means, we can better understand those who first settled here and the myriad phenomena that shaped their lives. The greatest of these forces is the inevitable element of change.

Seneca Heritage

SENECA OIL SPRING: A great deal has been written on the Seneca Oil Spring on the Seneca Reservation near Cuba, New York. However, it is necessary to add a few words about twentieth century changes at the site first discovered in 1627. The claim is made that the spring is the oldest oil discovery on the North American continent as so indicated on the maps of French missionaries from present-day Quebec. To commemorate the three-hundredth anniversary of this discovery, the New York State Oil Producers Association erected a bronze plaque briefly explaining this claim. The plaque is embedded in a large boulder near the fenced in pool. Today, the Oil Spring Park is maintained by the Allegany County Department of Public Works and is open to the public.

THE OLD COUNCIL HOUSE: This is one of the oldest buildings in Western New York dating from the mid 1700s. Currently located in Letchworth State Park, this famous structure originally stood in the Town of Caneadea on Council House Road. Approximately twenty to thirty Seneca homes stood back from a high bank overlooking the Genesee River, and its central feature was the Old Council House. It was built of hand-hewn logs a foot or more thick, neatly dove-tailed at the corners, their crevices packed with moss chinked with clay. Its length was fifty feet and the width twenty feet. It was roofed with "shakes" or large, split shingles with an opening for smoke to escape. At one end was a rude stone fireplace and doors on opposite sides.

An early white settler, Joel Seaton, used it for his dwelling. He also moved it closer to the river. In later years it was used as pig barn and fell into a severe state of disrepair. About 1870, John Stearns Minard

◄ *Seneca Oil Spring about 1900*

Seneca Council House at Caneadea, circa 1870

collaborated with William Prior Letchworth to take prompt measures for its rescue and preservation. It was subsequently moved to Mr. Letchworth's estate. On October 1, 1872, the Council House, now in its new location, hosted the last Indian Council Fire on the Genesee. The days of the Senecas using the Council House for tribal meetings, conferring with the British during the French and Indian War and planning attacks on white settlers stealing their lands were over.

Late twentieth century technological studies have shown the Council House was built by the British in the mid-1700s, perhaps in an attempt to discourage the Senecas from going to Fort Niagara. These studies have further shown the corner post notches were British military style, the fireplace is not of Seneca origin and some carvings on the interior logs were similar to Germanic runes. Serious doubts have also arisen that the current roof is not in keeping with the era. To date, no Carbon-14 dating or dendro-chronology studies have been undertaken.

Near the original site of the Council House sits a large boulder with an embedded bronze plaque. The inscription on the plaque commemorates the 1782 "Running of the Indian Gantlet" by Major Moses Van Campen. The Catherine Schuyler Chapter, Daughters of the American Revolution, dedicated this monument in 1908. The meandering Genesee River washed away the grounds upon which the Council House stood. The monument is on private property commonly known as the Estabrook Farm and is clearly visible from the road.

Highways of the Past—Indian Trail Trees

About 2002 Lee and Donna Ryan of the Almond Historical Society found an intriguing photograph in the society's archives. The photograph, taken in the early 1960s, depicted an unusually shaped tree locat-

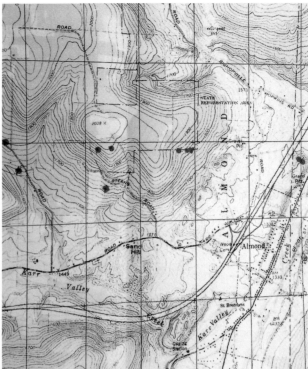

Left: Indian Trail Tree in Almond

Right: Global Positioning System Map of known trail trees in the Town of Almond. The two "lower" trees point north to main trail trees that point east to the Canisteo River in Hornell. These lower two trees are located on very small streams running to Karr Valley Creek. Each dot marks the location of a trail tree.

ed on Bully Hill Road in the Town of Almond. The tree was very large with one branch bent at a right angle to the trunk several feet off the ground. With their curiosity piqued, they conducted computer research and discovered such trees are believed to be the oldest living historical landmarks in the country. They are found in the eastern half of the United States.

It is believed the Indians bent tree limbs to indicate which direction to go through the dense forests, where to find water and perhaps shelter and a good place to ford creeks and rivers. The Indians would select a hardwood sapling, prop up a low branch with a thong or forked stick (perhaps similar to a "white man's tongue") and weigh the end down with a sinew cord. The tree branch would then grow upwards at the end and the tree would become permanently disfigured. Other branches growing horizontally on the limb would be removed thus forming the nose indicating the direction of travel. After Indians started traveling by horse, they made the deformed branch higher, enabling them to better see it. This type of tree is called "a horse and rider tree."

As of March 2005, the Ryans have located and identified over fifty such trees in primarily eastern Allegany County. They are mapping tree locations using GPS technology with their goal being twofold: a better understanding of Indian trail routes and also placing markers on these trees, thereby informing people of their significance in hopes of their preservation.

Our Nineteenth Century History Updated

THE VAN WICKLE HOUSE: This Greek Revival–style architecture dwelling at 30 West Main Street in Angelica, built in 1802, is the oldest house in Western New York. Evert Van Wickle, recruited

by Philip Church and Moses Van Campen to explore and survey a tract of 100,000 acres, was one of the first settlers in Angelica. It has been determined lately that this house is the first framed house built west of Bath, Steuben County. Today the house is owned by the Rod Glasspoole family.

THE OTTO MIX LOG CABIN: In 1804, John Crawford built a log cabin on Crawford Creek Road in the town of Caneadea near the hamlet of Oramel. A well-known local artist named Otto Mix owned the cabin before it was acquired by Richard Klein of Cuba in 1982. He moved it to his property on South Street for preservation. It is believed to be the last pioneer log cabin still standing in the county. The Klein family also purchased and relocated to their property an early New England–style saltbox house. The house was built in 1824 on the Jordan farm on the Haskell Road. Both structures are in fine condition.

MOSES VAN CAMPEN HOME: This stately Georgian-style house east of Angelica on County Road 16 was built in 1809 of bricks made on the premises by Major Moses Van Campen. At the time, there wasn't another house like it within a hundred miles. Sadly, it fell into a state of semi-disrepair until Richard and Marilyn Warner purchased it in 1975 and started extensive repair and remodeling work. With a deep love of history and a strong sense for accurate restoration, they restored the house and literally saved it. Newer living quarters were added in the back but the front is architecturally in keeping with the 1809 Georgian style. They retired from this labor of love and sold the house to William and Denise Hart in 2001. In addition to being committed to further restoration work of the house, the Harts are also working to save the large, old barns on the property.

THE ALLEGANY COUNTY FAIR: The County Fair claims to be the oldest continuously operated fair in New York state having started in1844. During the time of the Great Depression and times of war, the Fair was still held, temporarily reduced in size. To celebrate the Fair's 150th anniversary in 1994, Ida Case and Judy Tyler updated the Fair's history. They wrote: "Every year, as surely as fruit and vegetables ripened and the frost was on the pumpkins, this sturdy perennial came to fruit, sometimes in September, sometimes in October, or late in August—bearing a choice collection of the county's pure-

Opposite page top: Otto Mix Log Cabin on original site in Oramel

Opposite page bottom: Van Campen House, Angelica, before restoration—the Victorian dormer and porch have been removed.

Above left: Governor George Pataki visits the Allegany County Fair, 2002. Left to right are Legislative Chairman Edgar Sherman, Assemblywoman Cathy Young, Governor Pataki, Bill Heaney, and New York State Agricultural Commissioner Nathan Rudgers.

Above right: Fair Board President John Cronk and his wife Lillian on right, presenting their "President's Award" to Jan Leathersich for her design of the County's Cornell Cooperative Extension booth, mid-1990s.

Top: "Ocean Wave" ride at the Cuba Fair, September 1908

Middle: Governor Charles Evans Hughes speaking at the Cuba Fair, September 10, 1909.

Bottom: Canal Warehouse in Belfast, Genesee Valley Canal bed on left, towpath and Pennsylvania Railroad bed on far left.

bred cattle, prize poultry, domestic exhibits, the best of crops, and trotting races." With the exception of 1854 when the Fair was held in Belfast, it has always been in Angelica.

One of the finest assets of the Fair today is its collection of steam-driven equipment. In 1964, Lynn Langworthy of Alfred trucked his 1920 model Baker steam engine to the grounds and the idea of a permanent steam display was born. In 1965, the first permanent steam display was started by Merel Case and Bud Wakefield. Carrol Burdick of Angelica was also a major contributor as he built many operating model steam engines. Another major asset of the Fair is the Pittsburg, Shawmut, and Northern Railroad Historical Society's depot and beautifully restored historic coach and passenger car.

The traditional appearance of a major country and western singing star or group on Friday night started in 1958 with the appearance of "Gentleman" Jim Reeves. The Fair is owned by the Allegany County Agricultural Society and is governed by a fifteen-member board of directors. The last two Society presidents have served with particular distinction: John Cronk from Fillmore, 1976 to 1999, and Martha Roberts from Scio, serving since 1999. Under their leadership major improvements have been instituted and construction of new buildings has taken place.

Cuba hosted the Valley Point Agricultural Society Fair that started in the late 1860s. The Whitesville Driving Park Association held a fair for many years that started in 1877. The Wellsville Fair was located where the elementary school is today. "Fair Street" leads from Route 417 to the school. Unfortunately, no reliable data exists as to when these fairs ceased operating.

THE CANAL WAREHOUSE: By the early to mid-1850s, the Genesee Valley Canal was finished to Belfast from Rochester. The building commonly called "The Canal Warehouse" was constructed in 1854 to ship hardwood from the county's forests to metropolitan markets. Its official name is the Rail and Titsworth Canal Warehouse. Over the years, the structure has been used for a variety of purposes. For many years it was used as a barn. During the construction of the Erie Railroad high bridge from 1906 to 1908, it was used as barroom with two murders taking place on its premises. About 1990, the Belfast Lions Club purchased the warehouse for preservation purposes. Considerable time and money was spent repairing the foundation and roof. They later sold it to Greater Allegany Preservation, Inc., which is continuing preservation efforts. The warehouse is considered the oldest standing commercial building on the New York State Canal System and in 2000 was placed on the State and National Registers of Historic Places.

Load of tanbark at the PS&N Station in Ceres, New York

CUBA LAKE AND DAM:

Cuba Lake was created by construction of a dam as a reservoir for the operation of the Genesee Valley Canal in 1858. It was the highest point on the Canal. At a point near the entrance to the canal a "Y" was constructed by which the waters could be diverted into either end of the Genesee Valley Canal. Thus, waters going in one direction flowed into the Genesee River, Lake Ontario, the St. Lawrence River, to the Atlantic Ocean; that which was sent the other way ran into Oil Creek, the Allegheny, Ohio, and Mississippi Rivers into the Gulf of Mexico.

When the Canal ceased operation in 1878, New York State, still owner of Cuba Lake, decided to make recreation the lake's primary purpose. About 1900, the State divided the shoreline into 289 perimeter lots and, subsequently, cottages started appearing. Of these lots, nineteen were located within the boundaries of Oil Spring Reservation. Treaties with the Seneca Nation in 1794 and 1797 created the Oil Spring Reservation including about fifty acres on present-day Cuba Lake. The Indian Non-Intercourse Act of 1776 forbids states from negotiating with aboriginal Indians without Congressional approval. There was no Congressional approval of the acquisition of Cuba Lake. The Seneca Nation felt that the lake was taken improperly and therefore brought suit to reclaim the fifty acres in 1985. In 1998, the federal court determined the state had violated the Federal Non-Intercourse Act when taking the Oil Spring property. As part of the settlement, cottage owners received the assessed value of their cottages, and the Seneca Nation received $20 million. As of early 2005, nineteen property owners forfeited their cottages to the Seneca Nation.

THE SOFT SIDE OF THE TAN BARK INDUSTRY: One of the first major industries in the Wellsville area was the harvesting of hemlock trees for the production of tannic acid obtained from the hemlock bark. Tannic acid was in great demand for tanning leather and the product was shipped out on the Erie Railroad. The industry was very productive from about 1870 until the depletion of the hemlock forest caused operations to cease by 1900. The pitfall of the industry became apparent many years later when numerous "soft spots" appeared in the streets of Wellsville. In the production of the tannic acid, the naturally occurring chemical tannin is removed from the bark. The "bark" is converted into a very soft, spongy useless commodity that was simply discarded in any low spot owners wished filled. The

Top: Angelica GAR (Grand Army of the Republic) members and townspeople gathered on the Library steps for a Memorial Day portrait in 1908.

Bottom: Belfast GAR (Grand Army of the Republic) Hall, "institute" in postcard message refers to the Women's Christian Temperance Union (WCTU).

places were unmarked and remain so today leaving street and building construction a game of "tannic roulette." Early Street was the site of a large tannery and perhaps this is why the street has traditionally been somewhat of a controlled roller coaster ride. Also falling victim to these unknown waste sites were the Trinity Lutheran Church on North Main Street in the very early 1980s, a North Main Street paving project in the mid-1980s, the South Main Street Bridge replacement over Dyke Creek, and most recently the construction of the new Microtel Inn and Suites on South Main Street was held up due to the discovery of tan bark.

THE GRAND ARMY OF THE REPUBLIC: Our American Civil War ended in 1865, and in 1866 veterans from the North formed a Veterans organization called the Grand Army of the Republic. Its purpose was to promote patriotism, comradeship, fraternity and the securing of pensions for their members. By 1900, this was one of the most politically influential groups in the nation. Every public-office-seeking candidate sought the endorsement of the GAR and this tradition continues today with candidates seeking endorsements from the American Legion, Veterans of Foreign Wars and Amvets Posts. The concept grew in the former Confederate States and was known as United Confederate Veterans. Each had auxiliaries with the Northern chapters known as Women's Relief Corps and the Southern chapters known as United Daughters of the Confederacy. Also, The Sons of Veterans was an auxiliary to the GAR. Veterans belonged to their local posts, state and national levels as well. Post numbers were assigned chronologically by each state and these posts were named after a soldier from that locale who died in the war.

The first GAR post in our county was Thorp Post No. 86 in Belfast, chartered in May of 1879, and its GAR Hall was built in 1887. The last surviving member of the post donated "his hall" unconditionally to the Town of Belfast in 1925 and it became the Belfast Town Hall. On July 4,1976, the current Belfast Town Hall was dedicated. It stands where the former GAR Hall once stood. The last post created in our county was chartered in September of 1889 in Allentown, Town of Alma. In this ten-year period a total of nineteen posts were chartered. Additional Posts were located in Almond, Cuba, Belmont, Wiscoy, Friendship, Bolivar, Richburg, Scio, Canaseraga, Stannards, Whitesville, Wellsville, Rushford, Alfred, Andover, Angelica, and Short Tract. Many posts secured heavy artillery cannons from the war and conspicuously placed them in front of their meeting halls. Most were given for scrap metal drives in either World War I or World War II. The only remaining GAR Hall in the county serves as the Friendship Community Center. The two large cannons in front are believed to be the last Civil War cannons in the county.

The GAR was also responsible for erecting many impressive Civil War monuments in our county. Perhaps the most visible is the one on the Park Circle in Belmont, dedicated in 1912 to the Civil War soldiers from the Town of Amity. Beautiful monuments are also located in Angelica, Belfast, Bolivar, Cuba, and Wellsville. The last Allegany County Civil War veteran to die was Dr. John A. Jones, a veterinarian from the Town of Allen. He died on May 10, 1941, at the age of 101 years. As the last plaintive echoes of "Taps" faded away over his gravesite on the family farm, the guests in mourning felt the end of an era, knowing he had at last joined his comrades "who tent on fame's eternal camping grounds."

John Stearns Minard: We would be very remiss if we failed to write about J. S. Minard, the first and greatest of our county historians. A native of Hume, Minard had extensive knowledge of the entire county, dutifully recording it in his many books on local history. It was said, business was not his forte and that he felt there were too many good stories to be gathered and written about. His major work was published in 1895–96 in conjunction with the centennial celebration of the first permanent settler in Allegany County, which honored Nathaniel Dyke who settled in Elm Valley in 1795. He called his book *Allegany County and Its People: A Centennial Memorial History of Allegany County, New York*. He also wrote the following books: *Life and Adventures of Major Moses Van Campen, Ye Old Log School House Tymes and Pioneer Sketches* in 1905, *Civic History and Illustrated Progress of Cuba, New York* around 1910, *Hume Pioneer Sketches* and *An Indian Parliament House and Its Last Council Fire*. He also wrote many papers and essays such as the history of the Church Family at Belvidere and sketches of Indian and pioneer figures.

After a lifetime of research and writing, Minard met a quiet and lonely end. While his life was full of personal disappointments, he always managed to be cheerful. Tragically, he lost his sight seven years before his death in 1920 and died while residing in the County Home in Angelica. He rests peacefully in Pine Grove Cemetery, Town of Hume.

RUSHFORD BAND WAGON AND TOWN BAND: Of the many venerable social institutions in our county, the tradition of going to Rushford for its Labor Day Parade and Celebration is eagerly

John Stearns Minard (Photo courtesy of Rondus Miller)

anticipated every year. This event dates to 1908 when the first parade was held to commemorate the town's one-hundredth anniversary. An integral part of the parade is the appearance of the Rushford Town Band being proudly drawn along the parade route by a team of beautiful Belgian horses. The Rushford Town Band was formed in 1857 and claims to be the oldest town band still in existence in the state. It acquired the present bandwagon in 1890. One hundred years ago, wheelwrights were readily available wherever the band traveled to play. Today, however, maintaining a wagon pulled by horses is a problem. The band relies heavily upon our area's Amish skill and craftsmanship for needed repairs.

FRIENDSHIP'S OCTAGON HOUSE: The octagon-style house of the mid-1800s is commonly called "Ink Bottle Design." Two octagons exist today in the county, the first on South Main Street in Alfred and the other on Salt Rising Road in the Town of Genesee. Both are privately owned and not open to the public.

Top: Rushford Town Band in front of old Rushford Academy, 1912

Bottom: Friendship's Octagon House in 1976

Friendship's Octagon House stood on Elm Street and was built in 1842 by John W. Hewitt. The most prominent owners of the house were Dr. and Mrs. Hyde. He was a homeopathic physician, and they were spiritualists practicing in the latter nineteenth century. The house fell into a severe state of disrepair in the mid-1970s. Philip and Glenda Carlson who lived next door, offered to purchase the property for $250 from the Town in 1976. They then donated it to the Genesee Country Museum in Mumford, New York. The museum moved the "Ink Bottle" house in 1987. Every piece of the house was painstakingly removed and numbered for the subsequent restoration effort on the museum grounds.

chapter 2

FARM AND HOME

Changes in farm and home life are of paramount importance in determining how we live in rural America. Perhaps nowhere else in our County is the element of change more graphic than with the rapid disappearance of traditional family farms once dotting our landscape. The life of a farm family in the first one hundred years of our county's existence was marked by a period of relative stability. This definitely can't be said of its second century.

When the pioneers arrived here in the early 1800s, forests covered the entire area. These forests gradually disappeared giving way to fields and meadows. By 1900, farms covered the countryside. However, change was looming on the horizon. The first element of change occurred in the Great Depression of the 1930s when hundreds of farms succumbed to foreclosure. During this period, New York State obtained thousands of acres of abandoned land that became the many state forests of today. The farms that survived did so only to face major problems starting in the 1960s, with the advent of innovations, inventions, and technological advances. These have brought about tremendous change in the field of agriculture. The size of dairy farms in particular has increased from an average of two hundred acres or less with about fifty milking cows to massive, automated farms with over one thousand milking cows. Most small family farms are no longer able to financially compete. Over the last half-century, succeeding generations on these farms have simply left the area or sought other types of employment. This in turn has brought about the closing of several dozen farm-related businesses in the county and, consequently, the loss of employment for hundreds of workers. The costs of conducting a farm business have exceeded the income of the traditional family farm. For the most part, their only choice is to "Grow large or sell out!"

Bearing testimony contrary to this trend is the arrival and subsequent success of the Amish in our county. Arriving in large numbers about 1970, primarily locating in the Belfast, Friendship, and Centerville areas, they have proven the viability of traditional agriculture practices by shunning modern technology. Their distinctive lifestyle might give credence to the belief that simplicity affords a peaceful existence.

◄   *Belfast Bakery delivery wagon, 1907*

This page: Ice harvesting on Andover Pond—note Erie Railroad boxcars ready for loading, circa 1910.

Inavale Grange Hall, Town of Wirt, in former cheese factory

Securing accurate numbers of working farms in the county is very difficult due to changes in the way various census numbers were gathered. Under the latest census format, these are the numbers of dairy farms in Allegany County as reported by Cornell Cooperative Extension, USDA: 1982—429, 1987—312, 1992—234, 1997—185, and 2002—175.

Rural Organizations

THE GRANGE: A clerk in the Agricultural Bureau in Washington, D.C., traveled to the South in 1866, soon after the Civil War ended. He was under orders from his superiors to determine the effects of the war on agriculture. Shocked by the ruinous condition of Southern farms and plantations, he sought to unite the nation in a brotherhood that would restore agricultural prosperity in both the North and South. Using an old English word for farm, he sought to organize the Grange. He failed in his efforts in the South but found fertile soil in Fredonia, New York, where Grange No. 1 was formed in 1867. Now formally known as the Patrons of Husbandry and patterning their ritual somewhat after that of the Masonic Order, the Granger movement expanded nationwide.

By 1900, the Grange was one of the most powerful and influential organizations in the country. Its lobbying efforts inspired the federal government to pass railroad regulations greatly benefiting farmers by equalizing shipping rates and encouraging dependable schedules. The Grange was instrumental in the establishment of Rural Free Delivery mail service in 1896. A high point in the life of the Grange in Allegany County occurred in 1905–06 when, with the help of adjoining county Granges, they successfully lobbied the New York State Legislature to establish one of the new State Agricultural Schools in Alfred. Today this is known as Alfred State College.

The Grange prided itself by stressing the idea of being a family fraternity with both sexes treated equally. Additionally it provided rural people with a social outlet and a means of exchanging beneficial agricultural information. This increased the popularity of the organization and by 1950 there were twenty-four Granges in Allegany County. Paralleling the declining number of farms in the county, its numbers have dwindled to only a few active Granges today. The remaining Granges play a vital role in their communities by helping local residents in various local needs such as food pantry drives, clothing drives, community benefits, and funding academic scholarships for students pursuing careers in agricultural related fields.

DAIRYMEN'S LEAGUE: Around 1907 dairy farmers in upstate New York united to increase their bargaining power by forming one of the country's first cooperatives—the Dairymen's League. Its purpose was to be politically active thereby benefiting dairy farmers. By the 1920s their membership had grown to more one hundred thousand farms. In 1923 the cooperative introduced the name *Dairylea* for its products. The Dairylea product line continued until 1988 when its commercial operation was sold.

THE GRANGE LEAGUE FEDERATION: Writing a brief history of various farm-related organizations is a formidable task as there were many small cooperatives competing with each other in the early twentieth century. However, in 1920, representatives from three leading cooperatives combined forces and created the Grange League Federation (GLF). This new corporation represented the interests of the Grange, Dairymen's League,

Representatives of different programs of Cooperative Extension in 1976: Left to right are Stephanie MacAfee, Home Economics; Marilyn Conner, 4-H; Lee Brumback, Ag Program; Kathryn Brown, Ag Associate; and Bruce Smalley, 4-H Program Leader.

and Farm Bureau Federation. In the 1920s, 1930s, and 1940s, GLF developed a complete fertilizer service including an efficient method for spreading lime, thereby enabling farmers to safely distribute sufficient amounts of this chemical to adequately restore the soil's needed nutrients. The dwindling number of farms in the 1960s claimed another victim when GLF became part of the Agway Company. Today, Agway is also struggling financially.

FARM BUREAU/COOPERATIVE EXTENSION: Allegany County Farm Bureau started in March 1913 at a meeting of the Allegany County Pomona Grange in Cuba. Officers were chosen with a constitution and by-laws being accepted. Among its many goals was achieving easier access for farmers to information on modern farm practices and management. It issued a quarterly publication called *The Farm Bureau Digest* which quickly grew into a monthly publication and was renamed the *Allegany County Farm Bureau News*. Today this publication is called *Allegany County Cooperative Extension News*.

Top: The first Soil and Water Conservation District building is in the middle of this mid-1950s photo. The photographer was standing in front of the present Belmont Fire Hall looking south on Route 19. The Belmont Erie Depot is on left. Felix Biancuzzo's service station is on the right.

Bottom: Typical busy morning at the Oramel Cheese Factory, circa 1910.

By 1917 a need was recognized for a separate organization to deal with issues of homemaking. In response, the Farm Bureau adopted a new constitution and name in 1920, becoming the Allegany County Farm and Home Bureau. By 1931, their programs had expanded, resulting in the hiring of a full-time agent in charge of Junior Extension work for the advancement of 4-H Clubs.

In 1955 a friendly separation of the Farm Bureau from Cooperative Extension took place. Farm Bureau became an organization for political advocacy and cooperative purchase while Cooperative Extension remained the unbiased source of technical and management information. Extension lost a highly regarded employee in 1989 with the retirement of seventeen-year 4-H Agent Bruce Smalley. When the executive director, Paul Westfall, transferred to Niagara County in 1998, Dianne Baker became executive director. Effective in 2000, Allegany and Cattaraugus Counties' Cornell Cooperative Extensions were officially combined under one constitution and one Board of Directors.

ALLEGANY COUNTY SOIL AND WATER CONSERVATION DISTRICT:

Allegany County became a soil conservation district by action of the Board of Supervisors on November 19, 1941. Its first meeting was held on January 21, 1942, in the Farm Bureau Office in Belmont, and Hugh Chamberlain from Caneadea was their first supervisor. The board currently meets at the Ag Service Center on County Road 48 in Belmont.

The District was formed to provide all county residents with information and facilities for the control and prevention of soil erosion, to promote better land use by putting all land to the purpose for which it is best adapted, to protect the tax base by protecting good land so it will not deteriorate and be abandoned, to reduce the cost of highway maintenance, to prevent floods and flood damage, and to improve the living conditions of farm families.

One of the myriad projects being undertaken by the District includes working with Trout Unlimited, private landowners, and the New York State Department of Environmental Conservation in coordinating the installation of riparian vegetation along stream banks to restore fish habitat. Another project deals with waste handling issues in agricultural districts and with overall agricultural operations.

The District is also involved with flooding and storm-water runoff concerns for communities, individual homesites and development sites.

The directors of the Soil Conservation District for 2005 are Hugh Wightman, Rodney Bennett, Mark Bainbridge, and Curtis Rung. Since 1980 Fred Sinclair has been the district manager.

Changes in Rural-Related Industries

CHEESE FACTORIES: By 1900 cheesemaking was one of the main industries of Allegany County. Cheese factories dotted the countryside, separated by only a few miles. During warmer months, safely and quickly cooling or processing their milk was a major concern for farmers. This led to the abundance of cheese factories in rural America. Some of the cheese factories were operated by various groups of farmers that hired the cheesemakers. Many factories were owned by individuals who hired the cheesemakers. Occasionally, factory owners made their own cheese. There were also several cheese dealers in the county. The worldwide price of cheddar cheese was established each week in Cuba. The words *Cuba, cheddar,* and *cheese* were practically synonymous as Cuba Cheddar Cheese was known all over the country.

The beginning of the end of cheese factories throughout the county came in the 1930s with the advent of electricity which allowed farmers to cool milk on their farms. This came about through the Rural Electrification Administration under the new federal government program initiated by President Franklin D. Roosevelt. This marvelous change was overwhelmingly welcomed by the rural people of Allegany County as an improvement in their lives.

CONDENSERIES: Early twentieth-century technology afforded local farmers a better way of processing their milk with the development of condenseries such as those operated by the Borden Company. They claimed their plant in Belmont was the largest of its kind in the state. The facility opened on May 1, 1920, and was located at the corner of Erie and Willard Streets adjacent to the Erie Railroad tracks. They built a siding off the main line that came in broadside to the loading platform and another siding opposite the plant to bring in coal cars. Most of the original building remains standing today with some of the Borden letters still visible on the smokestack. The purpose of the plant was to manufacture butter and powdered milk. During the World War II years, the plant also manufactured powdered lemon mix.

Peak employment reached almost two hundred. A decline in business came when Dairymen's League members in the area decided to transfer their milk to larger facilities in Arkport, Steuben County. Bulk tanks came into use on farms, and farmers found this collection method much more efficient. The Belmont Borden's plant soon became unprofitable to operate, and it ceased operations on February 1, 1963. Only seven employees worked there at the end.

Vanishing Americana: The Story of Barns, Silos, and Outhouses

Perhaps there are no better symbols of rural America than picturesque barns, silos, and the occasional outhouse. These symbols of the past are becoming more rare as time marches on, exacting its toll of abandonment and disintegration. Fires caused by spontaneous combustion of stored hay have also contributed to the loss of barns. A few large barns have been converted into living quarters today, creating a unique style of home architecture.

Four pictures of a barn's demise on Route 243, west of Rushford:
Clockwise from top left: 1988, 1990, 2001, 2005

BARNS: Farmers traditionally took great pride in their barns. In the late 1800s, the size of barns had to increase to accommodate greater quantities of hay pitched into the loft for winter feed, reflecting the increasing size of herds. Surely it was a rural status symbol as well: "the bigger the barn, the more successful the farmer." These massive barns became somewhat obsolete perhaps as early as the 1920s due to technological advances in farm machinery. Farmers were now able to make compact bales that took up less space in the barn. Their net result was having the same quantity of hay but less space needed to store it. Any new barn built would now be smaller.

One of the latest technological advances on our farms is the introduction of machinery capable of making massive round bales of hay conspicuously wrapped in white plastic. These bales can be stored outside with loss due to exposure being minimal. Fresh hay is chopped and blown into lengthy white plastic wrappers as well. Barns today are smaller and designed for equipment storage, maintenance shops, shelter for young stock, etc. Separate metal pole barns are constructed specifically for milking where computer controlled machines handle all phases of the milking operation.

Without a doubt, the most famous barn in our county is the Block Barn on South Street in Cuba. Originally called McKinney Stables, its official opening was June 10, 1909. McKinney, after whom the stable was named, was the greatest sire of 2:10 trotters in his day. The Czar of Russia once sent a mare so the McKinney strain could be added to his stable. The barn is 347 feet long by 57 feet wide and roofed with Celadon Terra Cotta tile from Alfred. Owner Bonnie Blair is currently restoring the barn.

Top: Tobacco ad on barn in Ceres, New York

Bottom: Famous trotter McKinney, as his new home, the Block Barn is being built. Blocks were made on premises. This was one hourse definitely not "rode hard and put away wet."

SILOS: With the size of farms increasing shortly after the end of the Civil War, farmers needed feed storage facilities large enough to hold a winter's supply. Just such a design was built in the Midwest in the 1870s with several places claiming its origin. The idea of a silo was born and spread rapidly throughout the northeast dairying region. Many early silos were built into the inside corners of barns while most remained outside but attached. Most of the early silos were square wooden types, but farmers quickly discovered problems as inside corners were difficult to clean and silage buildup contributed to crop spoilage due to little air circulation associated with the design. Farmers soon adapted and the round, wooden silo came into being. In some cases round silos were retrofitted into square ones. Octagon-shaped silos were also constructed and are very rare today.

New technology and design soon resulted with brick, ceramic tile, cinderblock, and concrete silos appearing in the early 1900s. Concrete soon became the mainstay. Shortly after World War II ended, a distinc-

Left: This very rare octagon silo is on the Chaffee farm, Town of Allen. Dr. Dan Fink, author of the classic book Barns of the Genesee Valley *is on the right.*

Right: Alfred-made terra-cotta tile roof outhouse, Town of Almond

tive, new design became popular. This is the blue "Harvestore" silo marketed by the A. O. Smith Company. Engineered to be mechanically unloaded from the bottom, these silos are insulated and glass-lined, giving the farmer airtight storage for better quality silage.

With silos serving as "sentinels on our landscape," they go hand in hand with traditional red barns as defining characteristics of our agricultural history. In time, they too will fall into oblivion.

OUTHOUSES: Hardly a dinner table topic of conversation, these venerable structures were of paramount importance to our forebears. Call them what you want: outhouse, backhouse, privy, johnny on the spot, back forty, etc., they played an essential role in people's lives. Outhouses, flushed aside by the invention of indoor plumbing, fit the bill.

The use of outhouses has progressed through the years defining a series of changes. Outhouses were in existence for centuries when "everyone had one" and thought nothing of it. This changed when indoor plumbing became a welcome reality. Many outhouses were subsequently removed thereby creating an invisible "status symbol" by virtue of their obvious absence. Today's surviving outhouses are sometimes used as toolsheds, storage facilities, and even as conversation pieces.

However, outhouses are not entirely obsolete. Outhouses have made a comeback in the latter half of the twentieth century in two areas of our county. First, they are mandatory for remote cabins and campsites where indoor plumbing is not practical. Secondly, the arrival of the Amish in the past thirty years or so, with their integral beliefs of shunning modern conveniences have again made outhouses a necessity.

This coal-burning steam-powered thrashing machine was owned by Bert Vosberg of Centerville, circa 1900.

Organic Farming

Societal changes over the last thirty years or so have made some people concerned about the flagrant use of pesticides, herbicides, and chemical fertilizers on the food they consume. People believing the cumulative effect to be harmful have created a demand for a chemical-free food supply. Organic farming has arisen to meet this need.

To be certified as an organic farm, the farmer must undergo a rigorous, yearly, on-site inspection of all equipment, animals, feed, fertilizers, milking procedures, cleaning agents and practices by a USDA approved certified agent. In addition, all trucks picking up milk and the subsequent dairy-processing procedures must be inspected and approved as well. Above all, the farm must not have any chemicals or foreign agents used in any way in the entire process to be considered organic. Currently, there are about a dozen organic farmers in Allegany County. One of the earliest farms to adopt organic farming requirements is the Charles Deichmann Farm in Phillips Creek, Town of Ward. The family became organic dairy farmers in 1974. It has been said: "the work is harder but the milk check is larger."

chapter

THE 3 R'S:
"READING, 'RITING, AND 'RITHMETIC" AND MORE

Elementary and Secondary Schools

PUBLIC SCHOOLS: According to our parents, when they were young, they walked several miles to school, each way, in especially deep snow, only to return home to do several hours of chores. Nowadays, kids ride a bus to school in relative comfort after being picked up near their home. They enjoy a comfortable classroom, can partake of a hot, nutritious meal and benefit from indoor plumbing, all usually taken for granted.

By 1900, there were at least 302 district schools in the county, mostly of the one-room variety. Paved roads in the 1920s and 1930s combined with the introduction of school buses, ushered in the era of centralization—the merging of one-room country schools into one large school located in the "central" part of the district. Most of the centralization was accomplished by the mid-1950s but some of the newer country schools held some elementary grades until the mid-1960s.

Centralization was achieved with much heartache and a few harsh words. For over a century, rural schoolhouses served as community focal points, a source of local pride and identity. Major change became inevitable when enrollments declined in places and operating costs increased. Centralization offered greater educational opportunities as the importance of having a high school diploma grew.

The latest trend in rural education in New York State is the idea of merging districts. The first merger occurred in the fall of 1940 when the Alfred School and the Almond School became Alfred-Almond Central School. Mergers in the 1990s have created Cuba-Rushford, Bolivar-Richburg, and Angelica merging with Belmont to become Genesee Valley. It must be noted there

◀ *Clarksville School, District No. 3, circa 1910*

This page: Phillips Creek School, Town of Ward, circa 1912

Above: Temporary Cuba school called "The Shack," 1910

Right: Wellsville High School, built in 1891, burned in 1909.

Middle: Bolivar Central School bus, 1938

Bottom left: Because the Wellsville High School burned in November 1924, the Class of 1925 Graduation was held in the Babcock Theater.

Bottom right: The rebuilt and remodeled High School opened in 1910.

were also consolidations of school districts. The Allentown High School was consolidated into the Scio Central School District in 1959. Elementary classes were held in the Allentown building until 1980.

PRIVATE RELIGIOUS SCHOOLS: Several have flourished for years in the county. Immaculate Conception School, originally called Sacred Heart, in Wellsville started in 1876 with the arrival of four members of the Sisters of Mercy. Today they have classes for K-8 with about 150 students enrolled.

HOUGHTON ACADEMY: This Christian boarding and day school separated from Houghton College in 1955. Construction of the present campus started in 1958 and today it has students in grades 7–12 on the main campus in Houghton. In 1999, a south campus was established in Belvidere for students K–6. In 2003, it relocated to the former Angelica Central School building and effective in 2005, its name became Centerpoint Christian Academy.

BOARD OF COOPERATIVE EDUCATIONAL SERVICES: BOCES established its offices on South Street in Belmont in 1962 with Andrew Haynes as superintendent. Thirteen county schools agreed to engage in the program. Vocational programs started in1966 in three existing buildings in Belmont. In 1967, a site was selected for a large campus on County Road 48. This facility opened in September of 1969 and today is called the "Andrew F. Haynes Occupational Center." Today the campus is part of the Cattaraugus-Allegany BOCES.

TRAVELING TEACHER: This program was started in 1970 by Mary Perkins from West Clarksville. After about ten years of volunteering her time and money to prepare individuals for taking the General Education Diploma (GED) exam, Mary was able to obtain funding through various sources including the New York State Division for Youth, Social Services, and private donations. Today, Southern Tier Traveling Teacher, Inc., under the leadership of John House, operates an in-home basic education/GED tutorial service for disadvantaged out-of-school individuals in Allegany County. Funding sources have also expanded and include Allegany County United Way, Youth Bureau, and Allegany County Community Opportunities and Rural Development (ACCORD).

Institutions of Higher Learning

Our county holds the distinction of being home to four separate institutions of higher learning: Alfred State College, Alfred University, Houghton College, and SUNY College of Ceramics at Alfred University with its two world-famous schools: School of Art and Design and School of Engineering. Few counties can equal the higher educational opportunities available here. These institutions have published recent detailed histories and also offer extensive yearly catalogs of course offerings and requirements. Therefore, it is not practical for us to reiterate the evolution and history of these venerable institutions. However, a few words are needed.

ALFRED UNIVERSITY: Alfred University was founded in 1836 by the Seventh Day Baptist Church, primarily as a school of theology. It was one of the earliest co-ed schools in the nation. Today, this four-year, co-ed liberal arts school is ranked as one of the finest northeastern institutions by the *U.S. News and World Report* with about two thousand enrolled undergraduates. Many graduate-level curriculums are offered. Nestled among the University buildings today, is the campus of the New York State College of Ceramics, administered by the University. Dr. Charles Edmondson serves as current president, having recently succeeded Dr. Edward Coll Jr.

Top: This parade in Alfred celebrated the passing of the Ag Bill in Albany.

Right: In April 2000 at the Spring Choral Concert at Alfred State College, President Dr. William Rezak, at right, presented the Silver Bowl Outstanding Service Award to Anthony Cappadonia, at left, for serving fifty years as choral music professor. At center is College Council President Augustus Filbert. In April 2005, Mr. "C" directed his fifty-fifth annual Spring Concert at the College.

Alfred University, Corning Glass Works, Allegany and Steuben Counties collaborated with the New York State Urban Development Corporation in 1987 to create a "Ceramics Corridor." The concept was designed to enhance the economic climate of the western and central Southern Tier regions by constructing two "incubator" facilities in Alfred and Corning. These buildings would provide space and amenities at a reasonable cost to fledging companies in the fields of ceramics and glass. It is now called the Ceramics Corridor Innovation Center.

HOUGHTON COLLEGE: In 1883, Houghton College was founded and today is affiliated with the Wesleyan Church. The college is a Christian, four-year, co-ed liberal arts institution with various graduate level programs as well. It has about twelve hundred students. On May 7, 2005, the college awarded its first graduate degrees to six Greatbatch School of Music students. Retired public information officer for the college, Dean Liddick, has written a recent history of the college called *The Chamberlain Years* in honor of President Dr. Daniel Chamberlain who has served the college for over thirty years.

ALFRED STATE COLLEGE: Alfred State College (ASC) had its beginning as a state school of agriculture at Alfred University (AU) in 1908 when it was created by an act of the state legislature. An important milestone in the history of ASC occurred in 1948 when it was incorporated into the newly organized SUNY (State University of New York) system. By 1952, Alfred State had achieved total independence from AU. Over these years, the campus of ASC gradually grew to occupy most of the hill on the other side of the valley from AU. Dr. Uma Gupta serves as current president, having succeeded Dr. William Rezak.

In 1966, an act of the New York State Legislature established a vocational center in Wellsville as a division of ASC. The campus is located on the site of the old Sinclair Refinery. The combined campuses of ASC have about thirty-five hundred students.

Public Libraries

Most of our current seventeen public libraries started in the late 1800s and early 1900s. Three were built with Carnegie Foundation monies—Alfred, Andover, and Bolivar. (The original Alfred Library is now owned by Alfred University and used for offices.) The Richburg Colonial Library has the distinction of being housed in the oldest building currently in use as a library. This building is Georgian-style architecture, having been built in the early 1800s. Most likely, the county's first library is the Wellsville Library having been started in the late 1860s. In 1910, a new, spacious David A. Howe Library opened on Main Street. Today this building serves as the Wellsville Municipal Building. Along the frieze over the windows are names of famous authors "carved in stone." The current David A. Howe Library opened in 1937. Mr. Howe, a native of West Almond, was a newspaper and industrial magnate.

For quite a few years, the public libraries of Allegany County have had computers available for patrons. Access to the Internet in this "information age" is another valuable service offered by our libraries. Inter-library loan of books is also available through the Southern Tier Library System.

Top: The cornerstone for the Bolivar Public Library was laid on Flag Day in 1910.

Middle: The cornerstone for the first David A. Howe Library in Wellsville was laid on July 29, 1909.

Bottom: The first Howe Library in Wellsville is now the Municipal Building.

"War is Hell," at least according to General Patton of World War II fame. No doubt he was correct, but he was also talking about those directly involved in combat. Our goal for this chapter is to briefly cover life on the home front during the wars and conflicts of the twentieth century.

World War I and on the Home Front

The "Drums of War" were sounding in Europe as early as 1914 with the United States entering the conflict officially in April 1917 when President Woodrow Wilson asked Congress to declare war "so that the world might be made safe for democracy." The patriotic spirit of aging Civil War veterans and fresh memories of victory in the Spanish-American War of 1898 encouraged tremendous numbers of volunteers to go "Over There." And they didn't come back 'til it was "over over there!"

This war from 1914 to 1918 was initially called "The Great War" and later, was referred to as "The War to End All Wars." With the advent of another global war about 1941, these two wars became known as World War I and World War II respectively.

SUPPORT FOR THE WAR: On the home front, the federal government quickly started raising the enormous sums of money needed to wage a modern war. A sure-fire way to do this was to convince the citizenry to loan their country huge sums by agreeing to purchase bonds. The First Liberty Loan commenced in May 1917, the second in October 1917, the third in April 1918, and the fourth in October 1918. A total of $19 billion, 40 percent over subscription was raised. A fifth drive garnered another $2 billion in funds destined for aid to weary allies at war's end.

In April 1919, a Whippet Tank visited Angelica in an effort to secure monies for the Victory Liberty Loan according to an article in the *Angelica Advocate*. The newspaper

◄   *Angelica Courthouse and soldiers drilling in 1918.*

This page: Medal given by Allegany County to veterans of the World War.

A Victory Parade was held in Wellsville on November 11, 1918, when the signing of Armistice ended the Great War.

reported three weeks later that the Town of Angelica alone had 164 subscribers who gave $50,850.00 and the Town of Allen with 11 subscribers gave $6,200.00. No doubt this was indicative of the patriotic spirit throughout the county.

SPANISH FLU: This virulent strain of influenza killed 21 million people worldwide from September 1918 through February 1919. In Buffalo alone, three thousand died. No known statistics exist as to how many died in our county; no doubt there were many. Deaths were caused by pneumonia that followed the flu. Wounded soldiers came home sick and the flu spread rapidly. Schools closed all over the country in addition to canceling church services and most other public gatherings. Public funerals were forbidden. An interesting aspect of this illness was that it affected young adults the hardest. As a result, orphanages were overcrowded in the following years.

THE AMERICAN LEGION: In May 1919, a few American soldiers stationed in Paris, France, formed a new veterans' group called "Comrades In Service." This was the official name for the 2.5-million-strong organization that would take its place in American veterans affairs as the ultimate successor to the Grand Army of the Republic and the United Confederate Veterans. The name was soon changed to the American Legion. (See chapter 7 for further details and other veterans' groups.)

VETERANS PARKS AND MONUMENTS: Soon after the Great War ended, many communities in Allegany County created Veterans Memorial Parks and also erected monuments. Such parks are located in Belmont, Cuba, and Wellsville.

O. P. A. Form No. R-306

UNITED STATES OF AMERICA
OFFICE OF PRICE ADMINISTRATION
SUGAR PURCHASE CERTIFICATE

Not Valid Before July 9
Date

Serial No. C 40088998

TRIPLICATE

THIS IS TO CERTIFY THAT:

Name: Mrs. Ralph Stockman   Address: 6 South

City: Friendship   County: Allegany   State: New York

is authorized to accept delivery of

_____ twenty one _____ (41) pounds of sugar
pursuant to Rationing Order No. 3 (Sugar Rationing Regulations) of, and at a price not to exceed the maximum price established by, the Office of Price Administration.

Date July 9, 1942

Local Rationing Board No. 2-3-1

By _____
Signature of issuing officer

County Allegany   State New York

Under Clerk-Stenographer
Title

To Be Retained by Original Holder

The Stamps contained in this Book are valid only after the lawful holder of this Book has signed the certificate below, and are void if detached contrary to the Regulations. (A father, mother, or guardian may sign the name of a person under 18.) In case of questions, difficulties, or complaints, consult your local Ration Board.

Certificate of Book Holder

I, the undersigned, do hereby certify that I have observed all the conditions and regulations governing the issuance of this War Ration Book; that the "Description of Book Holder" contained herein is correct; that an application for issuance of this book has been duly made by me or on my behalf; and that the statements contained in said application are true to the best of my knowledge and belief.

X Elizabeth O'Brien   [Book Holder's Own Name]
(Signature of, or on behalf of, Book Holder)

Any person signing on behalf of Book Holder must sign his or her own name below

and indicate relationship to Book Holder _____

_____
(Father, Mother, or Guardian)

☆ U. S. GOVERNMENT PRINTING OFFICE I 1942   16—28561-1   OPA Form No. R-302

UNITED STATES OF AMERICA

War Ration Book One

WARNING

1 Punishments ranging as high as *Ten Years' Imprisonment or $10,000 Fine, or Both*, may be imposed under United States Statutes for violations thereof arising out of infractions of Rationing Orders and Regulations.

2 This book must not be transferred. It must be held and used only by or on behalf of the person to whom it has been issued, and anyone presenting it thereby represents to the Office of Price Administration, an agency of the United States Government, that it is being so held and so used. For any misuse of this book it may be taken from the holder by the Office of Price Administration.

3 In the event either of the departure from the United States of the person to whom this book is issued, or his or her death, the book must be surrendered in accordance with the Regulations.

4 Any person finding a lost book must deliver it promptly to the nearest Ration Board.

OFFICE OF PRICE ADMINISTRATION

No. 487591 -335

Certificate of Registrar

This is to Certify that pursuant to the Rationing Orders and Regulations administered by the OFFICE OF PRICE ADMINISTRATION, an agency of the United States Government,

(Name, Address, and Description of person to whom the book is issued:)

O'Brien (Last name) Elizabeth (First name) Ann (Middle name)

462 (Street No. or P. O. Box No.) Gridley St. (Street or R. F. D.)

Buffalo (City or town) Erie (County) N.Y. (State)

5 ft. 7½ in. (Height) 134 lbs. (Weight) Brown (Color of eyes) Brown (Color of hair) 19 yrs. (Age) Sex {Male / Female ☒}

has been issued the attached War Ration Stamps this 7 day of May, 1942, upon the basis of an application signed by himself ☐, herself ☒, or on his or her behalf by his or her husband ☐, wife ☐, father ☐, mother ☐, exception ☐. (Check one.)

Nanette Lancaster (Signature)
(Registrar)

Local Board No. 14-1-1 County Erie State N.Y.

Stamps must not be detached except in the presence of the retailer, his employee, or person authorized by him to make delivery.

| WAR RATION STAMP 28 | 26 | 24 | 22 | 20 | ■ | 16 | 14 | 12 | 10 | 8 | 6 | 4 | 2 |
| WAR RATION STAMP 27 | 25 | 23 | 21 | 19 | ■ | 15 | 13 | 11 | 9 | 7 | 5 | 3 | 1 |

Top: Sugar Purchase Certificate from the World War II years. (Courtesy of Bette Stockman)

Middle and bottom: This War Ration Booklet was used to purchase necessities by Elizabeth O'Brien was from Scio while she attended nursing school in Buffalo. She is now Bess Mulligan from Belmont. (Courtesy of Frank O'Brien)

43

ARMISTICE DAY: At the eleventh hour of the eleventh day in the eleventh month of the year 1918 World War I ended on what became known as Armistice Day. This day became a legal holiday in 1938. In 1953, the name was changed to Veterans Day.

Heavy Artillery from Belfast given for the war effort proved the citizens were of high caliber.

ALLEGANY COUNTY HONOR ROLL: According to the *Belmont Dispatch* of October 27, 1922, the official Roll of Honor of the citizens of Allegany County was filed in the County Clerk's Office. It listed forty-eight deaths in World War I.

World War II and on the Home Front

World War II saw 16 million Americans in uniform stationed around the world. Most Americans had never heard of Pearl Harbor, Hawaii, until emergency radio broadcasts in the afternoon of Sunday, December 7, 1941, when Japan attacked U.S. military bases. "A day," President Franklin Roosevelt said, "that will live in infamy." On December 8 in his address to Congress, he asked for a declaration of war. Congress immediately obliged by declaring war on Japan. After Germany declared war on the United States on December 11, 1941, the United States became involved in a war on two major fronts that would last until 1945.

While industry was producing implements of war at full capacity, a united effort on the home front began. Most all aspects of life were affected: critical items needed for the armed forces were rationed, scrap metal was collected, and Victory gardens were started—even in cities. Everyone's focus was on helping to win the war. Generally speaking, "doing without" was the norm.

While U.S. soldiers were fighting in Europe or the Pacific, life on the home front was anything but normal. Probably the greatest single change on the home front was the active role of women. With so many men in uniform, many women went to work in factories, with the name "Rosie the Riveter" becoming an American icon of the war effort. It must also be noted that women now had two jobs—one at the factory and the traditional one in the home. Many women also entered the armed forces.

- The *Andover News* reported in their January 15, 1942 edition that the Allegany County Home Bureau was taking a survey of homes in the county that could take in evacuees from New York City in the event of an attack.

- As in World War I, the U.S. government sold "War Savings Bonds." This practice continues today only they're called "Savings Bonds." For May of 1942, the U.S. Treasury Department set a quota of $122,100 to be raised in our county by asking for 10 percent of all wages. A small advertisement in the May 7, 1942 issue of the *Alfred Sun* stated: "Your own quota is 10%, lend your country 10% of your pay or have the Nazis and Japs take (not borrow) 100%!"

■ In May of 1942, the *Andover News* reported that the county had ordered a blackout from 10:00 p.m. until 10:30 p.m. with all lights to be out, traffic stopped, all persons off the streets and people were not to use the telephone.

■ The *Belmont Dispatch* of August 20, 1942, stated the cannons (Civil War era) from the Belfast Park were taken to Buffalo to be melted down for the war effort. The cannons from Belmont went as well.

■ In September 1942, members of the Beta Sigma Phi Sorority held a fashion show on the steps of the David Howe Library in Wellsville and initiated the wearing of "warsages" made of war savings stamps.

■ On February 5, 1943, the *Wellsville Daily Reporter* quoted Lou Burton, county 4-H agent, telling the County Board of Supervisors in his annual report that "crops of the Victory Garden Program had a cash value of over $100,000 last year." Victory gardens sprouted everywhere.

■ The *Alfred Sun* reported in October 28, 1943, that fifty-six hundred acres of potatoes were harvested in Allegany County by over one thousand boys and girls who had been released from school for that purpose.

■ The *Northern Allegany County Observer* reported that in 1944, children were urged to collect milkweed pods as the milkweed floss was an ideal substitute for kapok, which was used in life preservers and linings in aviators' flying suits. One child alone in Fillmore collected over fifty bags. Enough milkweed pods were picked in New York State in 1944 to make life saving jackets to float 125,000 fighting men.

Top: This crowd attended dedication ceremony of Richburg's World War II Honor Roll, circa 1942.

Middle: Richburg Honor Roll sign

Bottom: Standard identification card for Ground Observer. (Photo courtesy of B.R.A.G.)

Top: Right after World War II, many veterans used their "G.I. Bill" benefits and went to college. Barracks-like housing units sprang up to accommodate these young, married students. Units similar to this 1948 photo of "Vetville" in Houghton were called "Diaper Hill" in Alfred.

Bottom: Tombstone of Donald Thompson and his co-pilot in Arlington National Cemetery.

It is impossible to determine the exact number of men and women from Allegany County who served in the armed services during World War II. However, we can make a very good estimate based on how many served from the Towns of Angelica and Wirt, as these towns published booklets a few years after the war ended in 1945. They showed photos, branch of service, rank, dates of service, and names of parents. The Wirt/Richburg booklet also included serial numbers, where they served, and medals earned. It included a special section listing the 8 men who died in service. The Angelica booklet honored its 170 who served while the Wirt/Richburg booklet honored 153. Alfred's Honor Roll at the corner of Main and West University Streets listed 145 names. Whitesville's Honor Roll listed 92 men.

Ground *Observer* Corps had many stations in the county from 1942 to about 1967. Volunteers spent countless hours in small shacks on hilltops. Observers had to call regional headquarters at Buffalo and report all aircraft sightings. Retired County Historian Bill Greene from Belmont was an observer and he said a typical report went: "This is Metro, Nectar 5, 1, Black. I have one bi-motor, very high, south of the post, heading southeast." This operation was eventually phased out due to quality radar.

Project Chairman Wally Harrier of Cuba, standing in center, addresses the crowd at Dedication Day. Dignitaries seated to his left are Kevin Collins, Tom O'Grady, Legislature Chairman John Hasper, Assemblyman Richard Wesley, and Congressman Amo Houghton.

On Memorial Day, 2004, many veterans and their families from our county traveled to Washington, D.C., to witness the dedication of the National World War II Memorial. A grateful nation finally acknowledged the sacrifices made by "The Greatest Generation."

The Korean Conflict

To those fighting in Korea, it most certainly was a war in every sense of the word. The period from June 1950 until July 1953 hardly stirred patriotic feelings of Americans back home. People on the home front were tired of war and its associated privations, so recently experienced. Veterans returned to an America that barely acknowledged their efforts and the Korean War soon became "The Forgotten War."

Only an armistice was signed, not a peace treaty to end the hostilities. In the fall of 2000, the Republic of Korea announced it would award its Korean War Service Medal to any soldier proving he/she was in Korea. Many such medals were awarded to Allegany County veterans.

Something happened in the country after World War II that profoundly affected the attitude of Americans towards war. The World War I era produced classic songs like "Pack up Your Troubles," "It's a Long Way to Tipperary," or "Keep the Home Fires Burning." Great songs of the World War II era include: "As Time Goes By," "I'll Be Seeing You," and "White Cliffs of Dover." During the Korean War, no one wrote songs one would later associate with the period.

The Vietnam Conflict

The Vietnam era of 1959 to 1975 would produce one famous song however; in 1966, Staff Sergeant Barry Sadler had a bestseller with the song "The Ballad of the Green Berets." Equally well known are the many songs of war protest, particularly from "Woodstock." Songs of protest would set the stage for the return home of Vietnam veterans, in many cases not as heroes but as pariahs.

The Allegany County Vietnam Veterans Organization (ACVNVO) proposed in 1983 that a monument be created on the County Courthouse front lawn to the men from the county killed in Vietnam. The legislators approved the idea in 1985 with legislator Delores Cross from Cuba and the county Employees Union giving the first monies. Scio schoolteacher/artist Tom O'Grady designed the central oval plaque called "Last Moment for Friends" while Kevin Collins of Collins Memorials designed the principle granite pieces of the memorial.

Grave of Corporal Jason Dunham, May 3, 2004.

The ACVNVO Memorial was dedicated on November 1, 1986, in a very moving, fitting tribute to the men who served their country. The monument consists of three different-sized sections. The left panel is devoted solely to honoring Allegany County's only serviceman missing in action—Lieutenant Commander Donald Thompson, a Navy pilot lost on February 4, 1967, near North Vietnam. Vietnam repatriated his remains in 2001 with positive identification in 2003. He was buried in Arlington National Cemetery with full military honors on September 22, 2003. On November 8, 2003, members of the Wellsville Legion Post honored Thompson by a ceremonial unveiling of a new memorial to him.

In the ACVNVO Memorial, the upright panel in the middle lists the names of the ten men from Allegany County killed in Vietnam. The horizontal panel on the right lists the names of nine men from the county who served in Vietnam and survived. The ACVNVO believes these nine men subsequently died due to complications incurred as a result of serving in Vietnam. When the monument was dedicated, they stated it was the first in the nation to do so. Since 1986, five more names have been added.

As World War I and World War II ended in joyous celebrations, the Korean War ended quietly, while the controversial Vietnam War will continue to be "fought" for many years. Fittingly perhaps, names may be added to this monument.

Recent Conflicts

In the African country of Somalia in 1993, an American helicopter was shot down while on a humanitarian mission. The pilot was Chief Warrant Officer Cliff Wolcott from West Clarksville, a 1975 graduate of Richburg Central School. Wolcott was killed and the retrieval of his body was the inspiration for the 2003 movie *Black Hawk Down*.

On September 11, 2001, the United States was senselessly attacked by enemy terrorists when four commercial aircraft were hijacked and flown into three high-profile landmarks—the World Trade Center Twin Towers in New York City and the Pentagon building in Washington, D.C. The fourth plane crashed in a remote area in Pennsylvania before reaching its alleged destination of Washington, D.C. Subsequent U.S. military actions in Afghanistan and Iraq stem directly from these attacks.

In March 2003, the United States invaded Iraq. Many military personnel from Allegany County were involved. Tragically, Corporal Jason Dunham of Scio died April 22, 2004, from injuries he suffered eight days earlier in Iraq. According to military reports, Corporal Dunham stepped between a live grenade and two of his fellow Marines. He was buried in Scio's Woodlawn Cemetery with full military honors on Saturday, May 1, 2004. With the loss of a native son, the reality of war was once again brought home to our county.

In April of 2003, Robin Green of Angelica started a local chapter of Blue Star Families of Allegany County. Membership is based on having a family member on active duty in the armed services. As a symbol of hope and pride, Blue Star Mothers display a banner with a blue star for each loved one serving. Should the loved one die, a gold star replaces the blue star as a symbol of sacrifice. Currently there are about twenty families involved.

chapter 2

PUBLIC HEALTH–HOUSE CALLS
TO HOSPICE

ALLEGANY COUNTY
1806–2006
BICENTENNIAL

Plagues, epidemics, pestilence, and similar maladies have been the bane of mankind for centuries. Early efforts to reign in these horrible problems had been minimal at best. Technological changes and the miracles of modern medicine have brought tremendous improvements to the health of the world's peoples. The vast majority of these life-saving changes, all too often taken for granted, have been discovered and implemented in the twentieth century.

By the end of the nineteenth century, scientists were in agreement that in order to protect public health, they needed to identify the various causes of diseases and how they were transmitted. The efficacy of vaccinations, the need for sewage control, and concerns for overall cleanliness were inherent in those efforts to protect the public's health. The evolution of public health care in Allegany County cannot be adequately addressed in exact chronological order, but a logical progression of developments in health care in the county is shown in this book.

About 1830, the Allegany County Board of Supervisors undertook the responsibility of building and operating the County Home in Angelica. Their intentions were to safely house and care for the county's indigent, homeless, and infirm residents. Until the "winds of change" prevailed in the early 1960s, the facility was a venerable institution. The decision was then made by the Board of Supervisors to close the County Home.

Nursing Homes and Residential Care Facilities

HIGHLAND NURSING HOME: This skilled nursing facility opened on Highland Avenue in Wellsville in May 1966. In its first two weeks of operation, it accommodated a total of one patient, who, needless to say, received everyone's undivided attention. Not long after it opened, two events occurred, contributing to its growth. First, the County Home Infirmary in Angelica closed its doors after over 130 years of operation. This meant bed space was needed for those displaced residents. For the first six months only private paying patients were accepted. Second, new federal programs were instituted allowing Highland to accept other patients. In response, Highland expanded to a forty-patient facility. In 1970, Wellsville Highland, Inc., became an eighty-bed facility. In 1994, they changed ownership and

◀ *General Hospital, Wellsville, New York*

became Highland Healthcare Center, Inc. The facility is currently owned by WHNH, Inc., a group of four investors from the greater New York City area. The current administrator is James Fuller, a Wellsville native.

In January of 1997, Highland expanded its services with the opening of Highland Day Services, Allegany County's only Medical Model Adult Day Care Center. They provide nursing-home-type services in a day care setting and transport clients to and from their homes throughout the county. They serve about forty clients on any given day. This facility is located on Chamberlain Street and the on-site program director is Kathy Parmenter, R.N.

WELLSVILLE MANOR: The newest nursing home in Allegany County opened its doors February 2, 1983, as the Wellsville Manor Nursing Home on Route 417 West. It is a 120-bed skilled-nursing facility originally owned by Dr. Joseph J. Tripodi and his children with Dr. Tripodi serving as first administrator. On April 19, 2001, the Manor was sold and assumed its current name. The current administrator is Reita-Sobeck Lynch. It is the largest skilled-nursing facility in the county providing short-term rehabilitation, long-term care, and hospice services.

MANOR HILLS: Manor Hills was built by the Tripodi family in 1989 as a forty-bed adult residential care facility, located behind the Wellsville Manor. In May of 1992 they broke ground for an additional forty-bed unit. In 1995, a third unit of forty beds was added and in 2000, a dementia unit. The current administrator is Cathryn Neugent and the facility is still owned by the Tripodi family.

WATERS OF HOUGHTON: In September of 1980, Houghton Nursing Care Center opened its doors and began admitting residents to its eighty-bed facility. The facility was owned and oper-

Top: Original Jones home/hospital with new maternity annex added in 1928.

Bottom: Jones Memorial Hospital in Wellsville, about 1952

ated by Nationwide Health Care Associates of Indiana. Its first administrator was Harold McIntire. In its early years, there was an active airstrip behind the building and it was a common sight to see small aircraft coming and going, much to the residents' delight.

In 1995, the Park Associates of East Aurora purchased the facility and renamed it College Park Health Care Center. At this point, full rehabilitation services began, involving physical, occupational, and speech therapies. In 2001 this one-hundred-bed facility was renamed The Waters of Houghton and is under the administration of Gary Narsen.

Hospitals of Allegany County

WELLSVILLE GENERAL HOSPITAL: In June of 1896, Francis E. Comstock, M.D. started his practice of medicine. As there was no hospital at that time, surgeries were performed in patients' homes. In 1909, a hospital was started on Harder Place but business soon outgrew the establishment, and with the help of Dr. Comstock, Wellsville General Hospital was opened at 92 Jefferson Street. This hospital, furnished through the generosity of local businessmen, had seventeen beds and stayed in existence until 1921. It closed due to its inability to "Keep up with the Joneses."

JONES MEMORIAL HOSPITAL: As its name implies, the hospital was named for its benefactors: William Folwell and Gertrude Fassett Jones. He made his mark in local politics rising to serve a term in the New York State Assembly. He later took an interest in banking and became the president of the First National Bank. He died September 9, 1910, leaving his estate to his wife. Upon her death on June 5, 1920, their home was willed to the community for a hospital with an endowment of $30,000. The gift was accepted by the Village of Wellsville on June 28, 1920, with the former Jones home being converted to a hospital that opened its doors on June 27, 1921. Her will stipulated the new facility bear her and her husband's names. During its first year of operation, 445 patients were admitted and twenty-five babies born. A barn on the property was remodeled as a laundry and housing for the nursing staff. The first addition was the new Tullar Maternity Annex, which opened July 16, 1928.

The 1950s began a new era. A modern, two-story brick building had been erected around the original Jones home, which was torn down upon completion of the new hospital on August 3, 1952. In 1968, a third floor was added to the center portion. A three-story west wing was added adjacent to the Genesee River and a two-story addition was constructed between the existing building and new wing. Then came Hurricane Agnes in June of 1972. The rain-swollen Genesee River overflowed its banks, undermining the new wing, causing its collapse into the raging torrent. No lives were lost and most of the equipment was saved. One of the few eyewitnesses, Mrs. Christine Boller described it as "quietly sliding into the noisily roaring river." Subsequently, a new wing was built from 1974 to 1975 using Federal Emergency Management Agency monies. After lengthy negotiations, the Hurricane Agnes account was finally closed in 1985.

Effective January 1, 1988, Jones Memorial Hospital became a not-for-profit entity, severing its legal ties with the Village of Wellsville. This change was deemed necessary to better enable the hospital to pursue various income sources not available to government agencies. In 1991, the hospital broke ground for a 44,000-square-foot addition on the east side of the existing building. On Monday, December 20, 2004, a ribbon-cutting took place opening the new maternity unit. This capped a major fund drive raising over $1.2 million to remodel the former maternity wing. Two days later, the first baby born in this renovated facility was Megan E. Babbitt, daughter of Richard Jr. and Michelle (Linza) Babbitt.

In their attempt to best serve the medical needs of the County, Jones Memorial Hospital has established a series of outreach centers known as the Jones Memorial Medical Practices in Belmont, Wellsville, and Alfred. The ones in Alfred and Belmont are both family practice sites while the Wellsville Loder Street location is dedicated to women and children's health services. The Bradley-Holbrook Medical Arts Building on North Main Street houses several medical specialists.

A very important part of the operation of Jones Memorial Hospital is the Auxiliary. The current Auxiliary, open to women and men, was formed in 1951 and consists of the following "Twigs" or branches: Evergreen and Hemlock from Wellsville, Lilac from Belmont, Maple from Andover, and Olive from mainly Wellsville and the Wellsville Business and Professional Women's Organization. In 2003 and 2004, the Auxiliary raised and donated $102,000 to the hospital. While holding many fundraising activities during the year, their two major events are the Gala Ball and Silent Auction in the spring and Country Fair in the fall.

FRIENDSHIP GENERAL HOSPITAL: This small facility opened April 4, 1919. The *Friendship Register* of April 10, 1919, said: "Friendship now has in actual operation not a sanitarium but a regular hospital and of such design and equipment and finish as to place it in a class with any of Buffalo's smaller hospitals." The facility was in a large brick former house on Sunnyside Street near the school. It had room and bed accommodations for sixteen people and the proprietress was Miss Donna Dobson, a graduate nurse of the Buffalo Homeopathic Hospital. The facility faithfully served the needs of the community for many years until the school purchased the building and used it for kindergarten in 1954–1955. The building was torn down in January of 1986.

Top: Friendship General Hospital in Friendship, New York

Bottom: Cuba Memorial Hospital in Cuba, New York

CUBA MEMORIAL HOSPITAL: A small privately run hospital opened on Spring Street in Cuba in 1908. This facility closed when the Soldiers and Sailors Memorial Hospital opened its doors on February 1, 1923. This new facility was funded by a popular subscription drive that raised $30,000. The original capacity of the new hospital was eighteen beds and eight cribs with 182 patients admitted its first year. The name was changed to Cuba Memorial in 1938 when the first addition was completed.

Genesee Country Hospital, south of Fillmore, New York

Improvements were made over the years and on September 7, 1952, a $300,000 addition was dedicated raising bed capacity to sixty-five. A major reconstruction project took place in 1967 when the current facility was built and the original Soldiers and Sailors Memorial building was torn down. This building consisted of four floors with a third floor long-term care facility. Its capacity was eighty-five beds with thirty long-term care beds. This $1.9 million expansion also increased emergency services and outpatient care.

The hospital constructed a 1,450-square-foot Cuba Family Health Center with physicians' offices adjacent to the main building. It opened for business on November 4, 1985.

In late 2004, Chief Executive Officer Andrew Boser III announced that Cuba Hospital was applying to the state to develop and build a continuing care residential facility. If this comes to fruition, it will provide independent living, assisted living, and skilled nursing services for senior citizens.

FILLMORE HOSPITAL: In 1930, Robert Lewis deeded the former Purdy farm on State Route 19, south of Fillmore behind the current Phillippi car dealership, to thirteen men for the construction of the Genesee Country Hospital also known as the Fillmore Hospital. The hospital was completed and opened in July. "Ripley's Believe It or Not!" was a popular newspaper column years ago. One of their entries stated the Fillmore Hospital was adjacent to a railroad crossing on one side and a cemetery on the other. The hospital was forced to close its doors on July 21, 1952, due to a shortage of patients and no surgeons on duty. The local weekly newspaper stated: "Fillmore was just too healthy to support a hospital."

Wellsville Sanitarium

An earlier institution once proudly graced North Main Street in Wellsville. This was known as the Wellsville Sanitarium, founded in 1904 by Dr. Virgil C. Kinney. Its purpose was the treatment of the sick. However, in an advertising brochure they stated: "The Well-Ville methods seem especially adapted for rheumatism and its allied conditions, the generally run down, tired out nervous wrecks and chronic invalidism." They further stated that Well-Ville is a practical institution rather than a fashionable resort. The brochure further stated: "Not a rest cure. Methods of treatment based upon an intensive elimination and physical upbuilding [*sic*]."

Top: The Well-Ville Sanitarium in Wellsville, New York

Bottom: The Allegany Sanitarium in Andover, New York

Offered treatments included: a simple quiet life and careful diet, judicious medical treatment, baths, salt rubs, oil rubs, massage, mechanical vibration, the use of electricity in all its applicable forms, and many other physical appliances.

About 1920, the Sanitarium expanded by adding nineteen new rooms, making a total of forty. On the roof they added a large solarium and three adjacent small rooms where patients could take their sun exposure alone. Dr. Kinney successfully operated the facility for almost thirty years and died in Florida in 1933. The facility stood vacant for about twenty years and then it was reopened as a hotel, bar, and restaurant. The structure was razed to make way for the relocation and construction of Trinity Lutheran Church, displaced by the effects of Hurricane Agnes in June of 1972.

Health Services

Prior to 1975 when the County Health Department was organized, health services were the responsibility of the state and were managed through a regional office in Hornell. The county had what was known as an "unorganized health district" with each town and village having its own public health officer. The officer was responsible for keeping records and statistics and, when warranted, calling for quarantines or issuing health bulletins. The county did have a home health agency consisting of public health nurses and a home care service.

The Health Association of Allegany County, 1917–1975: Many of the health problems of society were once the concern of private, volunteer organizations and government involvement in these issues only occurred under the prodding and pressure of those volunteer organization. In Allegany County, many of the early activities of the Association became services provided by the local government. The direction this organization would eventually take can be largely attributed to the leadership, foresight, and perseverance of its first leader, Catherine Codispoti Manis of Belmont.

The Association was founded in 1917 as the War Emergency Committee on Tuberculosis. The focal point of the Association's work was the prevention and cure of TB. During its first year, the Association hired a nurse who made house calls, provided doctor referrals, arranged for placements in sanitaria, and provided instructions for families caring for 105 TB patients in Allegany County. During the first years of its existence, the Association received donations from the American Red Cross and also relied heavily on Christmas Seals campaign funds. Seals were first sold in 1907 with the official name Christmas Seals For Tuberculosis Relief. The county also contributed monies to the Association. Among its many contributions to health improvements in the county, the Association provided hot lunches for needy children in rural schools and sought to mandate the inspection of dairy herds supplying milk to stores. They also hired a social welfare agent, the first social worker in the County.

In March 1926, this committee and Allegany County Welfare League joined forces and became the Allegany County Public Health and Welfare Association. During the 1930s the Association's executive secretary also served as probation officer and supervised probationers from Children's Court, County Court, and Justice Court. In 1936, children's welfare work became the responsibility of the Allegany County Welfare Department, and county employees were appointed to provide the required services. During the Great Depression of the 1930s, the Association became involved in helping other organizations with the distribution of flour and cotton goods to those in need along with distribution of relief vouchers. They were also involved with old-age relief.

The Children's Health Camp owned and operated by the Allegany Health and Tuberculosis Association, Inc., was located on a hillside at the east end of Cuba Lake. The camp was established about 1922 to give better health to undernourished, physically underdeveloped, and sickly children. Support came from private contributions and an appropriation by the County Board of Supervisors. It operated for a period of eight weeks in the summer and was open to children between the ages of five and twelve. Their facilities included eight cabins, a swimming pool, and a large playground. The first year the camp served 30 children and in 1942, there were 225 children.

The varied pursuits of the Association—tuberculosis prevention and cure, child-welfare, old-age relief, mental health, heart disease, hearing loss, and various lung diseases had been part of no set plan or predetermined blueprint. They came from grass-roots efforts lodged in Allegany County soil and grew as local needs and conditions dictated. They were indigenous to this area and dedicated local citizens worked hard and long to make Allegany County a healthier place to live. For fifty-eight years the Health Association provided residents of Allegany County with a multitude of services and worked to improve the public health and welfare of the community. This history of the Association embodies within it a parallel history of developing governmental responsibility.

ALLEGANY COUNTY HEALTH DEPARTMENT: The County Health Department, as we know it today, started in 1975 primarily as a result of a growing number of sanitary code problems. Without an organized district, which a department is, the county had no means of enforcing sewer system requirements, restaurant cleanliness, etc. On February 27, 1975, a resolution establishing the department was approved unanimously by the county legislature. The first public health administrator was Margaret Connelly who had been serving as head of the public health nurses. Also created at this time was the County Board of Health. Charter Board members included: Dr. Eisenhardt, Alfred; Dr. Taylor, Cuba; Dr. Nystrom, Houghton; Dr. Tartaglia, Wellsville; Doris Halstead, Cuba; Legislator Don Kramer, Whitesville; and James Warner, Portville.

Once the County Department was formed, it was up to the individual village or town to decide whether to discontinue their health officer position and join the county district. Most of them joined the County district, but the villages and towns of Alfred and Wellsville opted to stay with their own system for the next year when they too joined the County district. Mandatory services in 1975 included enforcing state public health laws, performing tests and follow-up checks for venereal diseases, tuberculosis, and other communicable diseases.

Conrad Kruger from Cuba served as director from 1978 to 1979 when David Dorrance from Scio was appointed director. Since its inception, the department has greatly expanded and now has about seventy employees. The two major areas of responsibility are nursing and environmental services, each offering a host of programs including: home nursing care, clinics, testing, inspections, educational courses and information, various permits, and technical support.

The current director is Dr. Gary Ogden. Members of the County Board of Health serving presently include County Legislator Ron Truax as president, Dr. David Brubaker, Dr. Leo Cusumano, Mohamad-Zahi Kassas, Timothy LaFever, Catherine Richmond, and Willard Simons, D.D.S.

HOSPICE: For most of the first half of the twentieth century, doctors made house calls. Today, county health department nurses make house calls. One of the most recent developments in home health care is the concept of Hospice, which is primarily involved with making house calls. Hospice is a nonprofit organization that provides medical and psycho-social care to terminally ill patients and their families. This is provided either in the patient's home or in an institution. While their headquarters had been established in Olean for several years, they opened an Allegany County office in 1991. It was located in the Belmont Grange Hall on Willetts Avenue with Dr. Tartaglia serving as first medical director. It was first known as the Comstock Hospice Care Network. Today, it is known as Homecare and Hospice Network with an office in Wellsville. House calls have truly evolved, lending credence to the old axiom that "history repeats itself!"

While compiling information for this chapter, miscellaneous items surfaced we found interesting and deemed worthy of sharing.

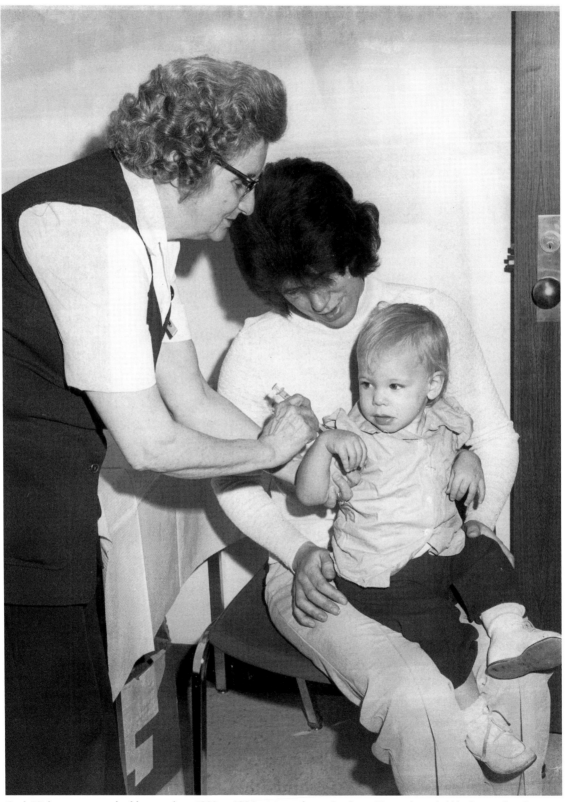

Ruth Nickerson, county health nurse from 1980 to 1986, giving a shot to Stephanie Harms being held by her mother, Joanne.

- In 1898, four mild cases of smallpox were reported in Cuba. A strict quarantine was enforced. Also that year it was reported in Fillmore that smallpox vaccinations were making about half the people sick and the general opinion was that "the smallpox would be preferable to being laid up by the vaccination."

- In 1910 there was a death notice for Dr. J. H. Pierce, a veterinary surgeon in Wellsville, who died in New York City where he had gone for treatment in the Pasteur Method. Having been bitten some time ago by a mad dog, he had waited too long after being bitten so there was no hope for him.

- In 1921 there was a scarlet fever epidemic in Belmont. A lady wrote: "Of course the children had to get it. So I was in quarantine along with the kids. My husband had to work so he couldn't come home."

- One of the most feared diseases of all time was polio. This viral illness paralyzed tens of thousands of children in the United States and half a million worldwide each year.

- In 1916, four cases of polio were reported, one each in Allentown, Andover, Angelica, and Wellsville. Two deaths from polio were reported at this time in Steuben County.

- In 1944 the opening of school had to be postponed for two weeks due to a polio epidemic in Cuba.

- In October of 1953, the last patient in the polio ward at St. James Mercy Hospital in Hornell was discharged. Total cases of polio reported since the July epidemic outbreak remains at 20 in Allegany County, 108 in Steuben and 67 in Chemung.

- In May of 1955, first and second grade pupils at Bolivar and Richburg schools will receive their first Salk antipolio shots. The "go ahead signal" came early this week from Dr. Milton Tully of Hornell, District State Health Officer. The series of shots had been scheduled for late April but were postponed when the Salk serum first came under fire following some polio deaths on the West Coast early this month. A total of thirty-five area youngsters were withdrawn from the projected inoculation program by their parents when nationwide criticism of the Salk serum forced the delay. Thankfully, the Salk vaccine given by injection and the Sabin vaccine given orally proved very effective and the dreaded disease has been eradicated in the United States since 1979.

chapter

WITH AND AGAINST THE LAW

WITH !

The vast majority of us are decent, law-abiding citizens who consider our various police agencies as friends upon whom we can call in times of need. In the 1800s and early 1900s, the only law enforcement in rural areas was the responsibility of the local constable and sheriff. About 1915, as automobiles became commonplace in the country, the need for "rules of the road" and their enforcement became apparent. Increased population, which led to increased number of complaints, inevitably, led to creation of additional police agencies.

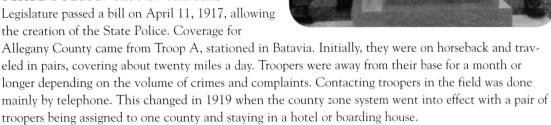

STATE POLICE: The New York State Legislature passed a bill on April 11, 1917, allowing the creation of the State Police. Coverage for Allegany County came from Troop A, stationed in Batavia. Initially, they were on horseback and traveled in pairs, covering about twenty miles a day. Troopers were away from their base for a month or longer depending on the volume of crimes and complaints. Contacting troopers in the field was done mainly by telephone. This changed in 1919 when the county zone system went into effect with a pair of troopers being assigned to one county and staying in a hotel or boarding house.

Motorcycles with sidecars were used in the 1920s along with horses, as few cars were available. Soon, cars were used solely. Starting about 1930, due to increased demand on the troopers, permanent stations in each county were established. The first station in Allegany County started in Friendship in December 1930. They moved to Route 417 west in Wellsville on July 18, 1945. Satellite stations have been opened in the following places to shorten response time: Belfast from 1953 to 1963, Fillmore from 1973 to present, and Almond from 1977 to present.

◀ *Cuba Chapter WCTU at a Cuba Camp Conference*

This page: Left to right at the dedication of the memorial to fallen State Troopers Rasmussen and Roy on November 16, 1994, are Major Pedro Perez, Sergeant David Gresham, and Sergeant Kevin Kailbourne.

A major change took place in December 2003, when the troopers moved their county headquarters to a new, larger, state-of-the-art facility in the Town of Amity, just south of Belvidere, almost in the middle of the county. This change allows a faster response to the increased number of calls on I-86.

One of the saddest events in New York State Police history occurred in Allegany County on September 8, 1927, when Troopers Rasmussen and Roy responded to a call in the Town of Caneadea on East Hill. They were met with gunfire and both were killed. This is the only time in State Police history when two troopers were killed in one incident. Today, a monument to Troopers Rasmussen and Roy proudly stands in front of the barracks in Belvidere. The members of the "Long Gray Line" who honored them have made sure that, although they are gone, they are not forgotten."

WCTU Monument at Park Circle in Angelica

AGAINST?

However, people being people, sometimes they don't always keep their actions on the right side of the law. Many protests in the twentieth century were legal actions against perceived government wrongs at the national, state, or local levels. The actions of defiance of the Prohibition laws, Suffragettes demonstrating for the right to vote, Ku Klux Klan, domestic violence, and the Nuclear Dump Fight are all examples of this phenomenon that wrought tremendous change in the county.

WOMEN'S CHRISTIAN TEMPERANCE UNION (WCTU): This organization can trace its roots to the 1880s when the Allegany County Prohibition Committee was active. Membership was strong in Alfred, Friendship, and Canaseraga as they hosted prominent speakers and programs that railed against "demon rum." Assembly Grounds/Camp Meetings sprang up across the county with a large facility built in Cuba. Its last Camp Meeting was held in 1904 and the buildings were sold with the auditorium ending up in Houghton for the Houghton Seminary.

One can only imagine what husbands did at home when their wives attended what they referred to as "Women's Constant Talking Union." Obviously their efforts were successful with passage of the Prohibition Amendment in 1919. Enforcing Prohibition laws proved almost impossible. It was said that more whiskey was available during Prohibition than was available when it was legal. Practically every settlement had at least one "speak-easy" where passwords like "Joe sent me" would get you inside and "bathtub gin" and "bootleg whiskey" were readily available. People could find out where these places were located simply by reading newspaper accounts of police arrests. Allegany Country was dry until the amendment was repealed in 1933. One town in the county remains dry today—Caneadea.

WOMEN'S SUFFRAGE: The Nineteenth Amendment was ratified on August 24, 1920, just in time for women to vote in a presidential election. The Allegany County Suffrage Party was formed in 1894.

Illegal still busted by Sheriff Ray Dare and deputies in May 1940 between Angelica and Almond. "The sun shines in the window but the moonshines in the basement."

Photos courtesy of Sue Clark.

One of Andover industries mostly 19 for girls though.

Left: Rochambeau Silk Mill in Andover was "mostly for girls though."

Bottom: KKK chapter was pictured in the 1917 Alfred University yearbook.

Annual conventions were held throughout the county with Cuba hosting the 1917 convention. An attendee at the convention wrote on the back of her program: "Women's work in wartime has brought equal suffrage despite a man's statement that women can not fight, therefore they should not vote." She further wrote that: "Women can not work for their country without working for suffrage. Heads we win, tails they lose."

KU KLUX KLAN (KKK): The "Klan" was very active in the county primarily in the 1920s. It must be noted that this period of Klan activity was markedly different than the days of reconstruction following the Civil War. During this period, the Klan's main focus was only against blacks. In the 1920s, the second incarnation of the Klan directed its activities against blacks, bootleggers, adulterers, Jews, pacifists, radicals, Catholics, and evolutionists.

A huge rally was held in 1925 in Wellsville that was attended by over eight thousand who each paid a quarter admission. Activities consisted of drills by both men and women in full regalia and speeches. The highlight of the rally was a Klan wedding performed that evening. A safe assumption would be that the bride wore white. Generally, the Klan in Allegany County was a social and moral force rather than being violent. However, cross burnings were common throughout the county. Henry Voss from Granger said "Folks were more scared of a cross burning than if anybody's building was burning."

"A PRISONER IN A PRISON WITHOUT BARS": Domestic violence in one form or another has been around for centuries. It had gone relatively un-prosecuted until the last few decades of the twentieth century. A national, landmark case, dealing with a virtually unknown defense called "the battered spouse syndrome," was tried in the Allegany County Courthouse in 1983. On February 25, 1983, in their home near Cuba Lake, Leslie Emick killed her live-in boyfriend, Marshall Allison, by shooting him five times in the head as he slept. Her defense attorney (his fee was paid for by the National Organization for Women) argued that his repeated multiple forms of abuse made her a captive and she was unable to escape, and thus felt completely helpless and trapped. This was one of the first times in the history of jurisprudence the words *battered spouse syndrome* were used.

After a three-week trial that drew national media attention, Allegany County District Attorney Patricia K. Fogarty, in her closing argument, simply stated that the victim was unable to defend himself and she should be found guilty. The jury returned a verdict of guilty of first-degree manslaughter. After an appeal, the case was plea-bargained to a lesser charge of second-degree manslaughter. The defendant moved to Delaware and all sentences were transferred with her and remain there today.

"MY NAME IS ALLEGANY COUNTY": On December 20, 1988, New York State announced
that the county was one of ten host counties, statewide, selected for possible location of an innocuously named low-level nuclear waste storage facility (nuke dump). This came about as a result of the 1985 Federal Low-level Radioactive Waste (LLRW) Disposal Act that stipulated each state must take ownership of its nuclear waste and build its own LLRW site or join a compact with other states.

A few citizens quickly reacted and a meeting was held at the Almond Historical Society Museum to form a protest group, soon called "Concerned Citizens of Allegany County" (CCAC). The idea of protesting grew rapidly as the dumpsite selection team had scheduled a public hearing in Belfast on January 26, 1989. Response was overwhelming as five thousand people attended. One of the protest leaders during his turn at the microphone urged the massive crowd to stand and led them in unison with foot-stomping and a hand-clapping chant of "Hell No, We Won't Glow. . . ." The Siting Commission members in attendance must have realized the depth of resentment and determination of the county's citizens to stop them, while the citizens realized how serious a situation this was to the future safety of their county. The stage for potential conflict was now set. The magnitude of Allegany County's "David" taking on New York State's "Goliath" was suddenly felt by all in attendance.

Dr. Ted Taylor at Belfast rally on January 26, 1989. Dr. Taylor was a nuclear physicist who helped develop the atomic bomb for World War II. He later became an anti-nuclear-proliferation supporter.

It has been said that once to every nation comes a moment of decision that profoundly affects its future. In the two hundred years of Allegany County's existence, that moment was on December 7, 1989, when Sheriff Larry Scholes met with high-ranking officials of the New York State Police—two inspectors and a colonel. After the initial exchange of pleasant greetings, their conversation turned serious—who would handle police duties when the Siting Commission members made visits to the county—the State Police or the Sheriff's Department? The State Police made it abundantly clear it was solely the Sheriff's responsibility. Sheriff Scholes, after stating he had no road patrol or enforcement officers, leaned forward and specifically replied: "Take this message back to Superintendent Constantine and Governor Cuomo from Sheriff Scholes— That's S-C-H-O-L-E-S. Sheriff Scholes says 'BULLSHIT!'" The die was cast!

In his excellent, definitive book on the entire Nuclear Dump Fight, Dr. Thomas Peterson of Alfred University quoted Sally Campbell, media coordinator for ACNAG, when she said on December 8, 1989: "The battle between the nuclear industry and the county will now take place at the sites in the cold of an upstate New York winter. This will be our Valley Forge."

CCAC felt it best to fight the Siting Commission through legal action. A few members peacefully formed another group to take a different course of action— Allegany County Non-Violent Action Group (ACNAG). This group would pursue its protests through acts of civil disobedience. Siting Commission members made several attempts in 1989 and 1990 to make on-site inspections of the three proposed dump locations—the Towns of Allen, Caneadea, and West Almond. All attempts failed when CCAC and ACNAG members

Top: Congressman Amo Houghton is interviewed for Channel 4 at a Belfast rally, January 26, 1989.

Middle: Protesters circled Siting Commission members in the Town of Allen on December 13, 1989.

Bottom: "Grandparents For The Future" are (left to right) Alexandra Landis, Roland Warren, Clarence Klingensmith, and Ermina Barber.

68

peacefully blocked their way. Many arrests for civil disobedience resulted, with all arrested protesters identifying themselves by saying: "My Name Is Allegany County!"

The denouement came on April 5, 1990, when commission members attempted to visit the Caneadea site. However, this time they came with about thirty-five uniformed State Police officers as intimidating escorts. Superbly executed maneuvers by "turtle-masked" ACNAG and CCAC members impeded their progress several times. The first delay was on the bridge on County Road 46 when six prominent senior citizens chained themselves to bridge railings. After a peaceful, lengthy "discussion," the venerable seniors were arrested and gently removed by Sheriff Scholes and the State Police. The Siting Commission members decided to walk the several miles to the site. Several strategically placed pieces of farm machinery slowed them somewhat. After walking a mile or so on a beautiful spring day, the commission members, surrounded by officers, were met by six mounted, masked riders. A tense, brief standoff ensued until an order was given to "Take 'em Down!" A few physical confrontations resulted with several riders being forcefully "removed" from their mounts. Thankfully, wisdom prevailed on the part of the police and all withdrew. Official videos of the day's events were on Governor Cuomo's desk that night.

"Mushroom Mask," tractors, and the Caneadea Bridge. The Grandparents For The Future were under the flag.

Shortly after, the governor ordered all work stopped in locating a dumpsite. But the story is far from complete. The initial Federal Act of 1985 was challenged in courts for years. Eventually, the case came before the United States Supreme Court in June 1992. The justices ruled by a 6-3 vote supporting New York officials that Congress went too far with their 1985 Act. The cases of *New York vs. U.S. 91-543* and *Allegany County vs. New York 91-558* show that the voice of the people made a difference.

When the Nuclear Dump Fight started, the entire county was in only one New York State Assembly district with the seat held by John Hasper of Belfast. Right from the start, Mr. Hasper (as did New York State Senator Jess Present) "went to the wall" to keep Allegany County free of nuclear waste. The dump issue was "resolved" shortly before the 1990 Federal Census was completed. As political jurisdictions are based on population, district lines are redrawn every ten years. Some political observers are of the opinion that John Hasper was the victim of Governor Cuomo's retribution as Allegany County was subsequently carved up and placed piecemeal into three Assembly districts, effectively putting Assemblyman Hasper out of office.

The amount of nuclear waste is growing at an alarming rate, as is the problem of what to do with it. Activist Jim Lucey perhaps summed it up best when he said: "I would consider it a victory in the battle, but we haven't won the whole war." The Siting Commission still exists but is no longer funded by the State. The Commission could easily resume its dumpsite search with new funding. *Editors' note—Were this to happen, the editors have complete faith in the belief that CCAC and ACNAG would be at full strength within an hour of learning about that funding action. Their readiness to act would be equal to that of April 5, 1990.*

69

chapter 7

INTERESTS OUTSIDE THE HOME
AND WORKPLACE

Working long hours, many times six days a week, afforded people in the 1800s very little leisure time. But times would soon change with the advent of the industrial revolution, the rising influence of unions, the growth of urban and suburban areas with the diminished number of farms, and the increase in the number of employment opportunities. With those changes, the amount of time not devoted to merely surviving or earning a living greatly increased.

The history of the early churches in Allegany County is well documented in both the Beer's and Minard books. The churches not only provided for the spiritual needs of the residents but also provided many social outlets. While many of the county's churches today can trace their roots to pioneer days, many new churches have been formed in the last half-century, primarily of the fundamentalist Christian movement. This has brought great change in worship practices. Some of these new churches have erected edifices, while others meet in members' homes or rented quarters.

With all their newly available leisure time, people's interests expanded outside the home and workplace, giving rise to myriad new organizations, entertainments, and diversions. Sadly, only a few that best illustrate the main criteria of this book can be mentioned; namely, criteria depicting elements of change that affected people countywide.

Fraternal Organizations

MASONIC ORDER: By far, the Masons is the oldest of the county's fraternal organizations. Its emphasis on ritual has been "honored" because later groups have also adopted rituals for their meetings. The Order proudly acknowledges fellow Mason George Washington as he used a Masonic Trowel in laying the cornerstone of the United States Capitol in 1793. Allegany County Masons presided over the laying of the cornerstone for the new Courthouse on July 20, 1938, and also the new County Office Building in November 1976. Traditionally, membership of the Masonic Order in rural areas relied heavily on farmers. Lodge meetings often started at 8:00 p.m. as that was the earliest its members were able to arrive after completing milking and other chores. The dwindling number of farm families combined with so many other recreational options available today has taken its toll on the Masonic Order. Many lodges

◀ *Rotary Club's One-hundredth Birthday Party on February 23, 2005. Left to right are Butch Fuller of Belmont, Madeleine Gazdik of Wellsville, Dirk Knapp of Belmont, Randy Ellis of Fillmore, and Jerry Jones of Friendship.*

in the county have closed in the last ten years or have merged with neighboring lodges. There are ten lodges active in the county today.

EASTERN STAR: The Order of the Eastern Star is an adoptive rite of freemasonry for women who are properly related to a Mason. There are nine chapters active in the county today.

THE GRANGE: Grange history is in Chapter 2.

ODD FELLOWS LODGE: This fraternal organization once flourished throughout Allegany County. Today, only one lodge is active, meeting in Bolivar. Their name is derived from an old English word for "oath." The Rebekah Lodge is for women and only the Wellsville chapter is active today.

ELKS LODGE: The only lodge of the Benevolent and Protective Order of Elks and its Lady Elks in the county is the Wellsville Lodge No. 1495. It was founded in 1925 and now has about four hundred members.

MOOSE LODGE: The Wellsville Moose Lodge was formed in 1925 and includes men and women in its membership of about one thousand.

Patriotic and Religious Organizations

AMERICAN LEGION: The oldest patriotic group in Allegany County was the Grand Army of the Republic (GAR) and its history is in Chapter 1. The Legion was formed by a group of officers at the end of the Great War in 1919 and is the world's largest veterans organization. Their goal was to have a powerful organization to lobby for veterans benefits, provide help for disabled veterans, perform community service, and promote patriotism. These new Legion Posts often used GAR Halls for their meetings. Posts are named after one or two soldiers from that community who were killed in the Great War. Wellsville's Morrison-Hayes Post dedicated their new three-story, $400,000 post home on June 10, 2000. There are ten posts in the county today and some also have Sons of the American Legion Posts.

Not all veterans are eligible to join the Legion. Years ago, Congress passed legislation limiting membership eligibility to honorably discharged veterans, who for the most part, served during times of war or major conflict only.

VETERANS OF FOREIGN WARS: Like the American Legion, membership in the VFW is also restricted. To be eligible, a veteran must have served overseas in a war zone during specific periods.

AMVETS: Like the Legion and VFW in concept, AmVets Posts were formed for veterans desiring membership in such an organization but were not eligible in the former two. Their requirements, simply, are having an honorable discharge and, like the Legion and VFW, have the desire to further the cause of patriotism.

DAUGHTERS OF THE AMERICAN REVOLUTIONARY WAR: The DAR chapter serving Allegany County was organized June 12, 1897, in Belmont. At its second meeting, they chose the name Catherine Schuyler Chapter as their official name in honor of the mother of Angelica Schuyler Church and grandmother of Judge Philip Church. Their history publication says that "she was a woman who so bravely bore her part in aiding and maintaining the freedom for which our ancestors were fighting."

Membership in the DAR is open to any woman proving that an ancestor served in the Revolutionary War. Main interests of the DAR include:

> Compile genealogical records of Revolutionary War soldiers.
> Locate and place markers on their graves.
> Further the cause of patriotism.

KNIGHTS OF COLUMBUS: The Wellsville Knights of Columbus "St. Joseph the Protector" Council, was formed in the fall of 1904. As a national Catholic men's fraternal benefit society, it was founded to render financial aid to members and their families and assistance to sick and disabled members and their families. Social, intellectual fellowship, and service projects to benefit all concerned are strongly encouraged.

Service Organizations

Traditional service organizations started in the early to mid-1900s strictly to help their fellow citizens with no thought of remuneration for volunteer service projects.

ROTARY INTERNATIONAL: The oldest county service organization is Rotary International, founded in 1905 by Chicago attorney Paul Harris. The first Rotary Club in Allegany County is Wellsville's having been founded in 1921. Three other clubs exist in the county today, namely, Fillmore—1941, Friendship—November 1955, Belmont—1959. The motto of Rotary is "Service Above Self."

EXCHANGE CLUB: The Exchange Club was founded in Toledo, Ohio, in 1917 by leading businessmen as a forum to "Exchange" business knowledge and ideas. The only Exchange Club in the county was formed in Wellsville in 1928, meeting in the Brunswick Hotel. Today its main service projects focus on children and their well-being.

LIONS INTERNATIONAL: On June 7, 1917, in Chicago, businessman Melvin Jones founded Lions International. In 1925, Helen Keller asked the Lions to become "Knights for the Blind," and today, both internationally and locally, Lions have become synonymous with working for the visually handicapped. The first Lions Club in the county was formed in Wellsville on January 8, 1942, with thirty charter members. The other Lions Clubs in the county with their charter years are: Canaseraga—1953, Alfred—1966, Angelica—1968, Bolivar—1970, Andover—1972, Almond—1974, Scio—1978, Belfast—1985, and Cuba—1985. The Lions motto is "We Serve!"

LIONESS CLUBS: The first Lioness Club in the nation was formed in 1975 with the first in Allegany County being the Wellsville Club in 1981. Bolivar Lionesses were chartered on February 15, 1986, and the Canaseraga Lioness Club was chartered in March 1969.

Sorority and Service Societies

BETA SIGMA PHI SORORITY: This sorority consists of four chapters in the Wellsville area with one hundred members from surrounding communities. The chapters are: Gamma Pi, Laureate, Preceptor Beta Upsilon, and Xi Alpha Omicron. They stress cultural improvement, self-enhancement, and area service projects.

DELTA KAPPA GAMMA SOCIETY INTERNATIONAL: The Alpha Sigma Chapter is the Allegany County chapter for this society of women educators. They seek to unite women in educational fields, support positive education legislation, and provide scholarships to women furthering their educational pursuits.

Water-Related Outdoor Recreation

Allegany County is fortunate to have many quality outdoor recreational facilities readily available most any time of the year. Activities range from quiet moments of personal reflection along a rustic wooded stream to viewing or participating in large public sporting events. However, we can only include a few.

GENESEE RIVER: One of the region's greatest assets is the Genesee River, coursing the length of the county. Usually appearing peaceful and receptive to many leisurely pursuits, it can quickly turn deadly like a lover scorned. Dangerous deep pools and currents have taken lives of unwary swimmers over the years.

Some of the major recreational uses of "The Genny" are swimming, fishing, and canoeing. The largest special event on the Genesee River each year is the very popular Wellsville Lions Club sponsored "Trout Derby," usually held the end of April. The Lions Club releases about four hundred trout with biodegradable tags. Everyone catching a tagged fish wins a prize. The New York State Department of Environmental Conservation stocks the Genesee River each year with brown and rainbow trout.

Start of Innertube Regatta at Jack Bridge

The Village of Wellsville is the only municipality in Allegany County utilizing the river for its water needs. Their water intake is located upstream from the Village near the Weidrick Road Bridge. The water treatment plant on West State Street across from the high school provides treated water to village residents and also six water districts.

CUBA LAKE: When the dam was constructed in the mid-1850s to provide water for the Genesee Valley Canal, it was said, that the lake created was the largest man-made lake in the world. (See Chapter 1) One of the best features of the rich history of Cuba Lake was the carousel in Olive's Pavilion that operated from 1933 to 1972. The carousel was manufactured between 1912 and 1915 by the Herschell-Spillman Company of North

Tonawanda, New York. It was first used in Wellsville at the Stadel Brothers home on East Pearl Street where they operated it each summer until 1929. They sold it to Olivecrest Amusement Park at Cuba Lake. It was dismantled and purchased by New York State in March 1975 for $20,000 and is the most expensive acquisition ever made for the State Historical Collection. The restored carousel proudly adorns the fourth floor Terrace Gallery of the New York State Cultural Education Center in Albany. It is in a permanent display called "Windows on New York." The State Museum spent $500,000 to restore the carousel and $2 million to erect the structure in which it is housed. Visitors to the State Museum can now ride the "Cuba Carousel" for free.

Top: Lake View House, Cuba Lake, 1910

Bottom: Olive's Pavillion, Cuba Lake, 1910

Today Cuba Lake provides fine public boating, swimming, and fishing opportunities. About 289 homes, cottages, and cabins line its perimeter and are privately owned. It is governed by the Cuba Lake Cottage Owners Association, Inc. (See Chapter 1)

RUSHFORD LAKE: Rochester Gas and Electric Company constructed Caneadea Dam (1926–1928) to provide water in the fall to generate electricity in Rochester when the water level in the Genesee River is usually low. The names selected were chosen to appease the adjoining Towns of Caneadea and Rushford as the dam is entirely in the Town of Caneadea while most of the lake is in the Town of Rushford.

Top: Lake Side Inn, Cuba Lake

Bottom: Cuba lake, early 1950s

This Dam Project did not come to fruition easily. Two well-established hamlets would have to be destroyed and ultimately inundated in the name of progress and eminent domain—East Rushford and Kelloggsville. Many of the displaced persons quietly took the remuneration and relocated nearby. One lady was heard to say: "I hold no regret in moving to a strange place, it's different when you know that no one else will live in our homes." Today, during the water drawdown months of winter, one can see the foundations of former homes, barns, and businesses. In the winter, maintenance and necessary repairs are performed on the dam, gates, etc.

Construction contracts were "let" in December of 1926 with work in earnest commencing in February of 1927. By February 1928, the dam towered 140 feet high and 600 feet across the Caneadea Creek Gorge, the gates ready to close. The lake filled in less time than expected-taking a little over four months. The first boat to ply the waters of the new lake was owned by Hugh Thomas and was named *The Swastika*. (Editors' Note: The swastika is at least three thousand years old and has traditionally been used as a symbol of good luck and fortune. When the lake opened, Hitler's use of it was *not* widely known. The Nazi version was an inverted form of the traditional swastika.) When filled, the lake is V-shaped with about ten miles of shoreline and over eight hundred cottages in the Rushford Lake Recreation District.

Caneadea Dam and Rushford Lake are each owned by their respective towns. The Rushford Lake Recreation District was formed in 1981 by a special act of the New York State Legislature for the purpose of accommodating the needs of the cottage owners. A volunteer board of five commissioners governs the Lake District. Three members of the Commission are elected by cottage owners and the Town Boards of Caneadea and Rushford appoint one member each.

MOORE MEMORIAL POOL:
This public facility is located on South Main Street in Bolivar and open for seasonal use to the public. The pool was built in the early 1940s by oil producer Raymond Moore and donated jointly to the Village and Town of Bolivar in 1949 by his widow Ethel.

VETERANS MEMORIAL POOL, WELLSVILLE:
Following World War II, the Veterans Memorial Pool, built by public subscription, was dedicated on August 27, 1947. The pool was built as a tribute to the men and women from Wellsville who served in World War II. A huge crowd witnessed the ceremony capped by attorney Ellis Hopkins conveying title of the pool to the Wellsville Central School Board of Education.

Top: Caneadea Dam Construction, May 28, 1928

Bottom: Rushford Lake with very few cottages

Superintendent Alden T. Stuart graciously accepted on behalf of the school.

Shortly after, Sid Miles was appointed director and various swimming and lifesaving classes were offered to all children throughout the county. A later director was Richard Tishlar and Jim Stein served as a swimming instructor for many years. All went well for many years and the pool became a summer institution in Allegany County. Parents would drop their kids off at 9:00 a.m. for lessons followed by a free swimming period from 11:00 a.m. to noon. The pool closed for about an hour, whereupon, kids would flock to Hank Graham's newsstand and corner store at Brooklyn and West Pearl Streets. Hank would always welcome the kids. The pool reopened around 1:00 p.m. and kids could swim until 5:00 p.m. for ten cents, eventually rising to twenty-five cents. Family passes were available for the season. A contemporary comment might be: this was one of the first "day-care" centers in the county.

The summer of 1971 was the last year of its operation. Plans for moving the Genesee River and the construction of the nearby arterial which would necessitate closing the pool were considered by many to be a

Veterans Memorial Pool, Wellsville (Photo Courtesy of Lee Gridley)

"done deal" before the Flood of 1972 struck. Hurricane Agnes and its effects sounded the "death knell" of Veterans Memorial Pool. Despite justified protests by area veterans, the pool soon closed permanently.

ALLEN LAKE: Allen Lake, in the Town of Allen, was built in 1958 as a private venture. The New York State Department of Environmental Conservation purchased this fifty-eight-acre site in 1963 and opened it for public use, primarily fishing. It has a handicapped accessible fishing dock.

Fore!!

To some, perhaps Mark Twain said it best: "Golf is a good walk spoiled." To others, golf is a passion and there are numerous quality courses in Allegany County accommodating those wishing to pursue this passion.

WELLSVILLE COUNTRY CLUB: The club opened on October 24, 1911, with 104 members. It purchased the former Coats farm and built its original nine holes. Another five holes were added in 1971. The remaining four holes were added in late 1974. The Flood of 1972 wreaked havoc on the low-lying course. Dedicated members essentially rebuilt many ravaged holes. Rated as one of the finest courses in Western New York, this private course is open to nonmembers at the discretion of the club pro.

BOLIVAR GOLF CLUB: The club started in 1941 but due to World War II, the clubhouse was closed to conserve gasoline. Regular golfing activities resumed after the war on their nine-hole course. It expanded to eighteen holes in 1998, and this public course is now owned by Robert Mallery.

ALLEGHENY HILLS GOLF COURSE: This family-owned-and-operated business has been in the Bruckert family since they purchased the former Priday farm and converted it into a nine-hole golf course, opening in 1960. Henry and Mimi started the facility and in 1990 their son Conrad and daughter-in-law Donna took over. The Turfside Restaurant was started in 1980 while the back nine was added in 1994. The facility is located on County Road 7B, two miles west of Rushford. It is open to the public.

6-S GOLF COURSE: This family owned business in Angelica, at Transit Bridge, started in 1965 by the Short family, parents William and Marsha with their children Larry, Anita, Alan, and Nancy. They converted some of their family farm to a nine-hole layout. It was increased to eighteen holes in 1969. Nine more holes were added in 1981 and their last nine were added in 1988. It is open to the public.

SERENITY HILL GOLF COURSE: The former Harold and Bernice Greene farm on East Hill in Friendship was sold to Robert "Pudge" Cooper, who opened the golf course in 1985. This nine-hole public course is managed by Sam Swift.

VANDERVIEW GOLF COURSE: In 1988, Phillip Brown opened the newest public golf course in Allegany County on his farm overlooking the Vandermark Road in the Town of Alfred. He sold the nine-hole course in 1999 to Tony Galeazzo who runs it today.

Other Outdoor Activities

DRILL TEAMS, DRUM AND BUGLE CORPS: The Belmont Fire Company organized a drum and bugle corps in October 1929. It ceased performing during World War II as many members served in the armed forces. It resumed performing and was active as a senior corps in the early 1960s.

The Wellsville Blue Devils Drum and Bugle Corps was in its heyday in the late 1950s and early 1960s performing over a wide area. September 17, 1985, marked the passing of this musical institution when their leaders Fran Slocum, Rose Weinhauer, Marilyn Hennard, Berwyn Hauser, and Jim Hennard turned their treasury over to the Wellsville Central School Marching Lions Band.

The Wellsville radio station WLSV's Rhythmettes Drill Team performed between 1958 and 1965. They marched in parades and county fairs throughout the area and their highlight was performing for Governor Nelson Rockefeller when he visited Wellsville. Their leader Judy Austin donated their remaining artifacts to the County Museum in Belmont and the Dyke Street Museum in Wellsville.

A junior drum corps from Allentown, called the Allentown Yellowjackets, was also performing in the 1960s.

EGGLESTON PARK/BRENTWOOD STABLES AND RIDING CAMP: This once thriving facility for girls resembled a scene from the movie *National Velvet*. The camp with manicured meadows and prancing thoroughbreds was located on County Road 43, also known as Brentwood Camp Road, in the Town of Angelica. Initially, Brentwood was established on grounds donated to Allegany County for recreation by Mrs. Eggleston from Angelica. During the Depression, the Works Progress Administration built the cabins and Eggleston Park. In 1946, Donald Morris purchased Eggleston Park from the county and renamed it Brentwood. Virginia Potter of Alfred University became the director. Brentwood was the former home of the Alfred University Equestrian Team. Their new Equestrian Center in the Town of Alfred, nearer the main campus, opened in 2005.

The camp advertised in major, nationwide publications attracting students from many states. Offered activities included: equestrian arts, swimming, archery, tennis, etc. Richard and Becky Backer purchased Brentwood in March 1990. For many years, the camp used an old Shawmut Railroad car for its infirmary. The car was painted white, inside and out. Mr. and Mrs. Backer donated this car, named *Clara*, to the Shawmut Railroad Historical Society. (See Chapter 8, Shawmut Railroad section)

WELLSVILLE DRIVE-IN THEATER: For decades, this unique architectural design was an icon on the American landscape. This certainly was true for the Wellsville Drive-In on Route 417 East with its 100-by-40-foot screen and parking large enough to accommodate seven hundred cars. The screen was thought to be one of the largest in the Eastern United States, weighing forty tons, supported by wooden beams and one hundred yards of concrete. The facility was built in 1968 by David and Larry Scoville of Geneseo and operated by their father Phillip. Linda and Ray Hunt then purchased it in 1982. The Hunts decided to cease operations in the fall of 2001, and the last picture show was *Planet of the Apes*, shown on September 9, 2001. Ironically, Larry Scoville dismantled the screen on May 23, 2002, using the lumber to build a house. The land currently houses a New York State Department of Transportation facility.

Tonight's Feature Movie Is

The turn of the twentieth century witnessed the end of traveling theatrical production companies, opera companies, minstrel shows, etc., and the first of the silent movies. Many local opera halls were simply converted to movie theaters and the public soon developed an instant fascination with "talkies." Movie houses opened throughout the county including: Andover, Belmont, Bolivar, Cuba, Fillmore, and Friendship.

Many times, early movie houses were simply converted storefronts, hardly more than a level floor set with chairs and a screen up front. These silent films rarely ran more than twenty minutes. Two of these in Wellsville were the Star and Family Theaters on North Main Street. The Lyric was a larger theater, whose sidewalk imprint can still be seen today in front of the Texas Hot on Main Street. Another major theater located on West Genesee Street was the Temple, which operated as late as the early 1950s.

Top: The Belmont Theater was on the second floor of the Amity Town/Belmont Village Hall.

Bottom: Old Fillmore Opera Hall and Theatre

Babcock Theater, Wellsville

In 1916, Charles Babcock came to town, purchased the buildings formerly housing Stoll's Tailor Shop and Manion Plumbing and constructed the Babcock Theater, a more elegant structure. About ten years later, the theater was sold but the name Babcock remained for many years. Today, it is called the Grand Theater.

In 1925, a young man named Alexander Litchard became manager and later owner of the Babcock, a post he kept for thirty years. Mr. Litchard capably described this era when he said: "Admission was a nickel then, and the Wellsville High School across the street would dismiss just in time for the 3:30 matinee every Wednesday afternoon. My girl and I used to go to the movie and then to Cretekos' ice cream parlor for two chocolate shakes, also five cents apiece. You just couldn't beat it for a good time."

The Roar of Engines, Clouds of Dust and Cheering Crowds

The sport of stock car racing became popular following World War II. In the mid-1950s and early 1960s, three tracks operated in Allegany County: Angelica Raceway, a one-third-mile dirt oval track located on the County Fairgrounds; Cuba Lake Raceway, a quarter-mile dirt oval track located on North Shore Road across from Olivecrest Pavilion and behind the roller rink today; the Wellsville Stock Car Speedway, a half-mile dirt oval track located on the old fairgrounds where the elementary school and athletic fields are today. In 1969, a one-third-mile dirt oval track opened in Allentown, located on Drum Road and called Drum Raceway. The track operated until 1979. In 1981, a track called Circle-K Speedway opened in Whitesville that was a one-third-mile oval dirt track. It closed in 1984.

The chief announcer at most of the area tracks, in their heyday, was Larry Dye from Cuba. His ability to accurately spot the correct positions of cars and announce the race has led to his being a spotter for "Fox News" and "NBC Sports" broadcast teams as they cover major races today.

Above: Cuba Lake Raceway. Left to right are unidentified, unidentified, Whitey Gorsuch, unidentified, Dean Layfield, and Forest Geffers, Dean's head mechanic.

Left: Dean Layfield

(Photos courtesy of Ford Easton)

Whenever, wherever, conversations are heard about local stock car racers and racing in the county, one name *inevitably* comes up, that of the legendary Dean Layfield. Dean was the first driver from the county to race in Daytona. To accomplish this feat in the mid-1950s, he drove his car to Daytona, placed tape over the lights, rolled down the windows and then raced in a Daytona 500. This was when part of the race was on its famous beach. He then drove the car home. Tragically, Dean was killed while racing at Perry Raceway in 1961 in his famous car No. 9/16ths. Dean was from Allentown and the patriarch of the famous Layfield family of racers. Dean's brother Bill is racing today along with many other family members.

No racing conversation would be complete without swapping stories about the most visible figure at these races: that of the famous starter, Andover's "Whitey" Gorsuch, clad in his white jump suit. And jump he did!! His trademark was starting the race on the track and while running towards the rapidly accelerating cars, jumping into the air and furiously waving the green flag. Sadly the racing world lost Whitey on December 1, 1996.

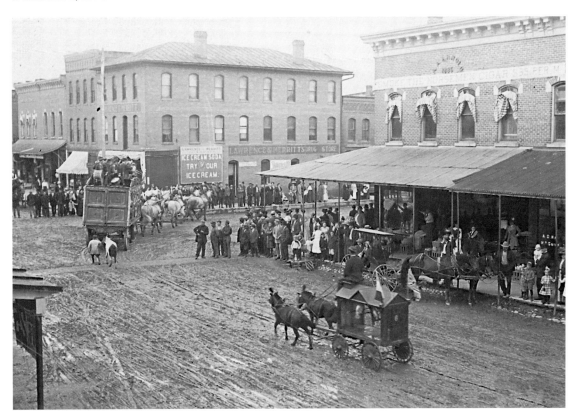

The circus comes to Cuba, August 1911

Up, Up and Away, My Beautiful Balloon!

GREAT WELLSVILLE BALLOON RALLY: The rally we know today started in 1976 at the airport on Niles Hill. It was called the Great Wellsville Air Show and consisted of one balloon, owned by Ray Zuczuski. The main feature of the show was a flight demonstration put on by Wellsville resident Ralph Twombley. A week before the show, Twombley captured the championship of his class of the Professional Race Pilot's Association at their national championship competition in Mojave, California.

The 1977 show was called the Great Wellsville Air Show and Balloon Rally with fifteen balloon participants. The combined show continued in 1978, but in 1979, the Great Wellsville Balloon Rally was ready to solo. That year, twenty-nine balloons participated and the rally was held at the former airport on Route 417, Bolivar Road. The rally moved to the Lagoon Field of Island Park in 1986 and now attracts about forty balloons each year.

chapter

EVOLUTION OF TRANSPORTATION

Power House of N.N.Y. & P. Traction Co. Ceres, N.Y.

One of the most significant events to occur in the history of New York State was the opening of the Erie Canal in 1825, connecting the Atlantic seaboard via the Hudson River with the Great Lakes. The Genesee Valley Canal operated through Allegany County from about 1840 to 1877. The arrival of the New York, Lake Erie, and Western Railroad in May of 1851 was the greatest transportation advancement in the county's history. The line was completed with the driving of the last spike in Cuba. The inaugural train carried Secretary of State Daniel Webster, a great orator, and Millard Fillmore, president of the United States. This was the only time a sitting United States president has ever been in the county.

The fierce desire for improvements in transportation was woven into the very fabric of American society. The stage was now set for the tremendous expansion of railroad and trolley facilities in Allegany County during the late 1800s, as this period was the height of the Industrial Revolution.

Clang, Clang, Clang Went the Trolley

In 1902, an established trolley line from Olean was extended east to Ceres, Little Genesee, and ended at Bolivar. This was the only trolley in Allegany County. It provided more regular and cheaper transportation than the Shawmut Railroad. Near Ceres, the line built its principal power plant, today known as the Coliseum, a roller-skating rink. To operate its electric cars, the plant generated its own electricity using massive gas engines that burned natural gas from company owned wells in the area.

Improved forms of transportation would soon exact a different toll. Paved roads, automobiles, and trucks able to carry freight took business from the trolley that ceased operations in 1926. The following year a bus service started.

◄ *The Trolley Power Station in Ceres was a roller-skating rink. It burned in the summer of 2005.*

This page: The first electric car entered Bolivar on December 11, 1902. Its last run was July 4, 1926. Newton House, shown here, was torn down in 1920.

Top: The final trip of the "Blue Bird Bus" in Bolivar was on November 5, 1949.

Left: Shawmut Depot in the hamlet of Burns, near Canaseraga.

Major Railroads in Allegany County

A comprehensive history of the railroads that have served Allegany County would comprise many books this size. Therefore, we can only briefly cover major lines of significance. During the oil boom days of the 1880s and 1890s, many narrow-gauge (a distance of 3 feet between rails) railroads were built in the county. Most went out of business for a variety of reasons. For the most part, railroads in the twentieth century were constructed to standard gauge (4 feet, 8.5 inches between rails).

PITTSBURG, SHAWMUT, AND NORTHERN RAILROAD: This railroad, formed in 1899, was comprised of five disconnected properties and seven financially struggling narrow-gauge lines traversing northern Pennsylvania and the Southern Tier of New York. The line ultimately ran from St. Mary's, Pennsylvania, to Perkinsville in northern Steuben County. Its intended purpose was to connect the coal mines with markets in the Northeast, yet it never touched upon any major industrial cities. Problems needing immediate attention included: changing from narrow gauge to standard gauge, reducing steep grades, and straightening portions of track. New track had to be laid to create one continuous line. The wooden trestle at Swains had to be filled and the iron bridge at Stony Brook had to be replaced.

87

Top: Horseshoe curve in Richburg heading to the "West Notch." Tracks and tunnel were removed in 1947 and a notch was cut through the old rail bed where Route 275 is today.

Middle: Part of Shawmut shops in Angelica

Bottom: Famous wreck of a PS&N coal train near Nile involving a head-on collision in September 1912.

The new line was hard pressed for money. In 1903, the line went into receivership and remained there until 1947 when it was forced out of business. By virtue of that fact, the line holds two records of dubious distinction in U.S. railroad history: the greatest number of years in receivership and the largest percentage of its life in receivership. Further complicating its operation was the fact their corporate offices were in St. Mary's and their maintenance headquarters in Angelica. This distance compromised their overall effectiveness. The death knell of the Shawmut sounded in 1946 when company doctor Betty Hayes complained to the federal government about deplorable living conditions on company owned properties in the St. Mary's area. The federal government finally realized the extent of their receivership status and forced them to cease operations. The end came in 1947 with the removal of tracks. At the end, the Shawmut had sixteen locomotives, eight cabooses, thirty-nine pieces of work equipment, and 106 freight cars, mostly hoppers.

Dubbed the "Pretty, Slow & Noisy," the PS&N Railroad was

the Shawmut railroad near Angelica, N.Y.

Shawmut "Funeral Train" taking up tracks on curve in Richburg, 1947.

taken to heart by the people it served. When in operation, the area around Angelica enjoyed economic prosperity due to the location of company maintenance shops. When the line closed in 1947, doom and gloom was predicted for the area. This did not prove to be the case however. The fascination this line held for the local people led to the formation of the PS&N Historical Society in May of 1981 with the encouragement of Jim McHenry from Angelica, who served as first president. The first vice-president was Bill Reddy. There were also thirty charter members. This dedicated group soon acquired an original Shawmut Coach No. 278 and has restored it to its original condition. The Allegany County Fair in Angelica granted permission to the Historical Society to build a one-quarter scale Shawmut Depot and relocate Coach No. 278 to the fairgrounds. Other cars were soon added to their holdings including an original Shawmut caboose that was constructed in the Angelica yards. Also donated was a private traveling coach, not originally a Shawmut car that has been restored by society members. This car is still called *The Clara*, named after Clara Higgins Smith, wife of Frank Sullivan Smith, an executive on the Shawmut. Its original number was No. 99 which the Historical Society has kept. *The Clara* was dedicated on June 7, 1998.

Remnants of the Shawmut can be seen in many areas along its old route. However, there are two places of significance; the famous horseshoe curve just north of Richburg on Route 275 and in the median of I-86 just east of the Friendship rest area. This railroad will live on in the hearts of those who appreciate the history of the Shawmut: "A railroad that started no place and ended no place with a lot of nothing in between." (Quote attributed to Paul Pietrak and others.)

BUFFALO AND SUSQUEHANNA RAILROAD: Commonly called the B&S, this railroad started out with great promise for the Western New York and Pennsylvania region and ended in bankruptcy. In the 1880s, Frank Goodyear, a wealthy entrepreneur from Buffalo, acquired rich hemlock forests in north-central Pennsylvania. He soon teamed with his brother Charles and formed an empire consisting of mammoth sawmills, coal mines, and a railroad linking the iron ore ranges of the upper Great Lakes with forests, mines, and steel mills of New York and Pennsylvania. A distinctive feature of the line was its quality construction with rugged seventy-pound rail built to standard gauge. Their roadbed, bridges, underpasses, and overpasses were constructed to highest standards of the time. A very distinctive feature of the line was its architecturally beautiful depots. Two B&S depots survive today and both are private properties. The Belmont Depot was moved from its original location on South Street near the old Belmont Central School to its present location on Willetts Avenue shortly after the line closed. The depot was converted into a residence and is currently owned by the Petrichick family. The Rushford Depot was moved about one hundred yards and is owned by Michael Ronan. It is now a workshop. Route 19 from Wellsville to Belfast parallels the B&S right-of-way, clearly visible in many places.

The line ran from Pennsylvania north to Wellsville. In 1902 it was announced that the line would be extended eighty miles to Buffalo. The first train using this extension ran on December 11, 1906. However, the death of Frank Goodyear in 1907 started a chain of financial events that forced the line into the hands of a receiver. Coal and coke traffic was diverted to the Pennsylvania Railroad and that removed the only reason for the continued existence of the B&S. In September of 1915, the Wellsville to

Top: The old B&S Depot in Wellsville stood across the street from the High School.

Bottom: Rushford B&S Depot

Buffalo section was sold and service was discontinued in 1916. The only track removed, was taken up north of Wellsville. A few locomotives and rail sections intended for Russia were diverted to France in the early days of the Great War. It is said, "All this equipment lies at the bottom of the Atlantic due to the help of one of the Kaiser's U-Boats." (From page 71 of Paul Pietrak's book on the B&S.)

WELLSVILLE, ADDISON, AND GALETON RAILROAD: In 1932, the Baltimore and Ohio Railroad acquired the remnants of the B&S. In 1955, they sold the old B&S division of their holdings to the Wellsville, Addison, and Galeton. Along with the right-of-way, they acquired the Galeton Shops, rolling stock, and six former B&S steam locomotives. Shortly after this transaction, diesel locomotives came into use. The WAG operated two trains per day, five days a week, becoming famous for its diesel oddities. The line adopted the slogan "The Sole Leather Line," for the tanneries served along the line. This much-loved local railroad met its demise in 1973, unable to recover from the economically crippling washouts on its line during the Flood of 1972.

PENNSYLVANIA RAILROAD: The Genesee Valley Canal closed in 1878. On the towpath, construction soon started for the Genesee Valley Railroad. Trains started running in 1881 and the line eventually became part of the Pennsylvania System. The Pennsylvania Railroad, at its peak, operated more miles of rail than any other line in the nation. The Olean-Rochester Division entered Allegany County at Cuba. The line had depots in Cuba, Belfast, Caneadea, Houghton, Fillmore, and Rossburg.

WAG Depot in Wellsville, old B&S depot is in the background.

In January 1962, the County Board of Supervisors received word the line would abandon its tracks in the county. The last train ran in the spring of 1963 and the track was torn up that summer. Today, its former roadbed is becoming the Genesee Valley Greenway Trail.

ERIE RAILROAD—RIVER LINE: In the very early 1900s, the main line of the Erie became very congested. Compounding the problem, the steepest grade on the entire Erie system was located between Hornell and Andover. This steep grade often required additional engines to enable trains to "make the grade." Frequently, trains were held up in Hornell to the east and Wellsville or Olean to the west just waiting their turn to climb the mountain. The highest elevation point on the entire line was at a place dubbed "Tip Top" in the Town of Alfred. Its elevation was 1,776 feet.

About 1903, the Erie Railroad started laying a parallel track in hopes of alleviating the effects of this "bottleneck." Due to narrow passes in the Alfred Station area, the attempt failed. An alternate route was chosen that necessitated building an entire new line from Cuba to Hunt in Livingston County. Called the "River Line or Cuba-Hunt Cut-off," an eastbound train could take this route at Cuba, traverse this new line to Hunt and then take the Buffalo Division line of the Erie to Hornell. There it would rejoin the mainline. A westbound train would simply do this in reverse. By utilizing both routes, the Erie no longer lost time and money due to the steep grade on the main line.

The chosen route of the River Line forced the Erie to erect two mammoth bridges for elevation compensation near Belfast and Fillmore. These bridges were built at the same time from 1906 to 1908. The "Erie High Bridge" construction at Belfast was not the only problem they faced in crossing the Genesee River Valley. Already in operation through Belfast were the B&S and the Pennsylvania Railroads. The only choice the Erie had was to cross over them, and this they did in grand style, erecting a bridge that quickly became a regional landmark. At the west end of the bridge, they had to build a wooden/earthen embankment, almost 1,000 feet long and at one end 65 feet high, enabling trains to be level with the

Opposite page

Top: Pennsylvania Railroad Depot in Cuba with Phelps and Sibley Mill at left.

Middle: Pennsylvania Railroad Depot in Houghton

Bottom: Pennsylvania Railroad Depot in Fillmore

90

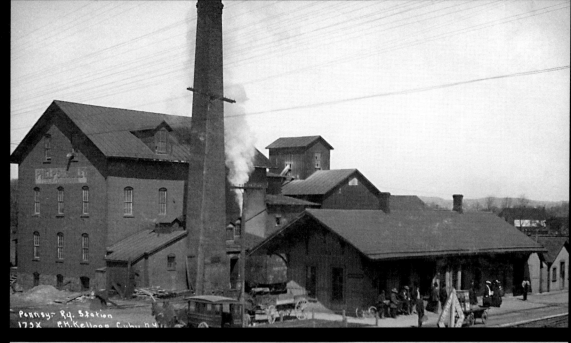

Pennsy- Ry. Station
175X   P.H.Kellogg Cuba. N.Y.

Top: Rossburg Hotel and Pennsylvania Railroad Depot

Bottom: Bert Smith from Wiscoy was a forty-year employee of the Pennsylvania Railroad. (Photo courtesy of Doris Harrington

Top: Photo taken from present-day Bristol Street in Cuba. "Our Lady of the Angels" Church is at right on Cherry Street. The Erie spur line to the Phelps and Sibley Mill is on the right.

Bottom: Erie train crossing the South Street Culvert in Cuba, New York.

Top: Erie train at Belvidere going under B&S bridge.

Middle: Track was laid "as they went" with this Hurley Track-laying Machine. Ties and rails were on flatbed cars with properly spaced ties coming by conveyor off an extension arm and rails were placed by hand. This scene is at the Erie cut-off at Cuba, New York.

Bottom: Erie Engine 2013 was wrecked at Belmont on November 7, 1909.

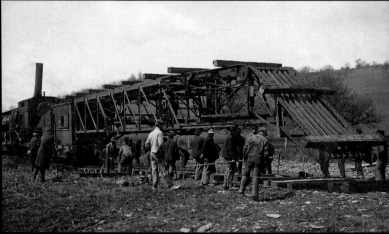

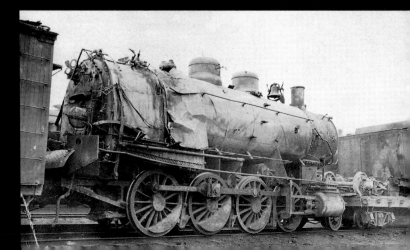

TRAIN9 WRECKED AT BELMONT 10-10-'19

Bottom: Erie Bridge surveyors with the west abutment in the background near Belfast, January 1907

Top: The relative size of the men in the foreground shows how impressive the Erie trestle was at Belfast.

Middle: Erie Bridge showing west abutment before the trestle was built.

Bottom: In the winter of 1907–1908 three railroads were meeting in Belfast. The Pennsylvania Railroad was in the valley going under the finished Erie Railroad Bridge in the background of this photo, while the Buffalo and Susquehanna Railroad went under the Erie in the foreground. The Erie embankment is in the center leading to the unfinished trestle.

Top: First test trains on the Belfast Bridge

Bottom: Erie Bridge near Fillmore over Rush Creek

bridge. The Belfast Bridge was 3,121 feet long and 141 feet above the river. The Fillmore Bridge over Rush Creek was a little shorter but taller. For construction of both bridges, materials were brought to the sites on the Pennsylvania Railroad.

The Erie Railroad did not fare well during the Flood of 1972, as a great deal of its roadbed was washed out. So extensive was the damage, a week after the flood struck, they filed for reorganization under bankruptcy laws. The end for the Erie came two years after the Penn Central Railroad, the nation's largest line, also sought reorganization.

CONRAIL: Extensive negotiations between the federal government and six failed railroads in the Northeast resulted in the formation of the Consolidated Railway Corporation, commonly known as Conrail, effective April 1, 1976. One of the greatest ironies in Allegany County's history occurred forty-five minutes into the life of Conrail—its first wreck. In the dark of night at 12:45 a.m., the sounds of crunching metal and grinding steel were heard in the streets of Cuba. The derailment of twenty-six cars caused the tearing up of three to four hundred feet of track. (April 1, how fortuitous!)

Belfast Bridge, ready for scrap, August 1981

Conrail detractors say the line "stumbled, fumbled, and bumbled" their way along, practically ruining the railroads in the Northeast. One of their first questionable practices was the demolition of all Conrail-owned buildings deemed not needed. In retrospect, this is viewed as a euphemism for tearing down depots and other historic structures. This they did with reckless abandon, making no offers of donating depots to local groups interested in preserving them. Local historical societies and several individuals in both Alfred Station and Cuba made purchase offers on depots in their communities. In response, Conrail countered with a $15,000 price tag for each. Instead of offering these beautiful, historic and structurally sound depots to those interested parties for the "proverbial one dollar," Conrail summarily destroyed them. The depots in Andover and Wellsville survived Conrail's wanton destruction only because the Erie had previously sold them. Conrail also came under a great deal of criticism for allegedly not providing timely service for shipment of large, finished products from local industries.

However, criticism of these practices paled in comparison to the objections they received over the demolition of the former Erie high bridges near Belfast and Fillmore in April of 1981. The hue and cry was heard far and wide, to no avail. The graffiti-laden beloved bridge at Belfast soon lay in a long line of twisted, tangled steel; sadly, now just a memory.

Conrail ceased regular rail service through Allegany County in the mid-1980s. On March 8 and 15, 1994, two of the last Conrail trains to use the old Erie main line backed into Wellsville from Olean to pick up the largest pre-heater ever built in Wellsville. The Ljungstrom Air Preheater was built for the Orlando Power and Light Company with the center section alone weighing over a million pounds. The units were shipped from the main plant on Route 417, east of Wellsville. Loading the flatcars however,

Whitesville Depot of the New York and Pennsylvania Railroad, the "NYP." The line ran from Canisteo to Shinglehouse, Pennsylvania, with Whitesville being the only location in Allegany County served by the line. It was shut down as a result of a washed-out roadbed from the Flood of 1935.

proved to be a problem. The massive, self-propelled railroad crane in the plant hadn't been used for quite a few years and the Preheater Company had to recall a few retired experienced crane operators for the job.

In spring 1997, Norfolk Southern Corporation and CSX Corporation agreed to acquire Conrail through a joint stock purchase. Approval was granted by federal regulatory agencies on July 23, 1998. The old Erie main line from Cory, Pennsylvania, to Hornell became part of Norfolk Southern who then leased this line in February 2001 to the Southern Tier Extension Railroad Authority. The line is operated under the aegis of the Western New York and Pennsylvania Railroad Company. The transfer took place April 9, 2001.

WESTERN NEW YORK AND PENNSYLVANIA RAILROAD: By early 1998, many people felt they'd never see regular train service again across Allegany County. Cuba native William D. Burt would soon prove them wrong. Mr. Burt is the driving force behind the Western New York and Pennsylvania Railroad and serves as president and chief operating officer. A major investment of nearly $25 million has been used for repair of major washouts, replacement of ties, installation of quarter-mile-long welded track along portions of the line and numerous other repairs. New or refurbished signals were installed at fifty-five crossings in New York and thirty-one in Pennsylvania. Most of the company's income today is derived from shipments of Pennsylvania coal to power plants in the Northeast.

Evolution of Roads In Allegany County

While stagecoaches were still the norm in the early 1900s, automobiles would slowly replace them. Travel on roads in the early 1900s could, at best, be described as "terrible." Dirt roads were quagmires when it rained, dusty and full of ruts when dry, and impassable many times in winter. Often the owner of a disabled auto was told by passers-by on a horse or in a wagon to "get a horse!" A road of logs laid side by side across wet or swampy ground was called a corduroy road. Another early type of road was the plank road that consisted of laying down planks of wood in hopes of creating a smoother surface.

The burgeoning number of automobiles by 1910 spurred the need for immediate road improvement. Even though Town Highway Departments had been around many years, the County Department of Highways was formed in 1909 to provide consistent, standardized construction and maintenance of roads. The New York State Department of Transportation was formed for the same reason, assuming ownership and maintenance responsibilities for roads bearing heavier traffic volume.

Fortunately Allegany County is endowed with massive deposits of quality sand and gravel, courtesy of receding glaciers of the Ice Age. Numerous sand and gravel mines are found throughout the county and have provided a nearby source of vital raw materials needed for road construction and paving.

The County Department of Highways established a repair and service headquarters in Friendship on Depot Street in 1921 and moved the shops to North Branch Street in 1934–1935. In 1921 they laid the base for the first hardtop county road that extended six miles from Nile to Clarksville that became County Road No. 1. This road was blacktopped in 1922 and was twelve feet wide. Standard width on county roads today is twenty feet minimum but now twenty-four feet is preferred. The county road numbering system is more or less based on the order in which the county assumed ownership of said road.

While it is not our intent to recite the history of the New York State Department of Transportation, several items of interest are worthy of mention. In the 1920s when many of the first state roads were being improved, it was a common practice to construct adjacent "rest areas." Roads were relatively poor, breakdowns and flat tires were common occurrences, and travel times were often lengthy; therefore, these rest areas were appreciated and utilized. They were taken out of service in the early 1990s. A sharp-eyed traveler can spot their locations in three places: 1) Route 244, three miles east of Belmont on the north side of road; 2) Route 21, Town of Alfred one-half mile south of Kenyon Road; and 3) Route 19, Town of Caneadea, a few yards north of the former Erie High Bridge abutments. In the 1950s the State Education Department placed a large historic sign in this rest area. When that area closed, the sign was relocated to the Interstate 86 eastbound lane rest area between Friendship and Belvidere.

In 1960, New York State Department of Transportation, utilizing a Federal Aid Reconstruction Contract, realigned and elevated Route 19 in Belvidere by using the old B&S abutments over the Erie tracks and Van Campen Creek. The same sharp-eyed traveler can spot the old B&S grade at numerous places in this area. One of the B&S abutments over the PS&N roadbed can be seen about three hundred yards south of the Route 19 bridge over I-86 in Belvidere.

Bridges of Allegany County

Allegany County has the distinction of being the only New York county having streams that drain into three major watersheds: the Allegheny, Genesee, and Susquehanna Rivers. Thus, one cannot travel far in the county without realizing the imperative need for the existence of bridges. With 122 bridges on county roads alone, it is not practical to mention more than a few structures that represent something of historical significance or important changes in bridge construction.

Top: Workers pave Main Street in
Angelica about 1915.

Middle: A large crew of men pave
Cuba's Main Street with bricks in 1912.

Bottom: Near Andover, circa 1930

Sylor Memorial Bridge, Angelica (Photo courtesy of Guy James, Allegany County Department of Public Works)

CANEADEA BRIDGE: This one-lane, steel and camel back truss bridge is the second oldest bridge still standing over the Genesee River. (Lattice Bridge in the Town of Hume is older.) On April 5, 1990, this bridge was the scene of one of the most significant confrontations between protesters and New York State in the famous "Nuclear Dump Fight." On that fateful morning, six venerable senior citizens chained themselves to the bridge. Their purpose was to impede the progress of the State Police escorting members from the Siting Commission as they sought to travel to a proposed nuclear waste disposal site. In 1993, when it was ninety years old, the County Department of Public Works closed the bridge due to safety concerns caused by erosion of abutment stones. A group of Caneadea residents led by Miriam Morton and Maxine Schembri organized the "Save The Bridge Committee" and initiated the town's Indian Summer Fest, in an effort to raise monies for their cause. On October 30, 2002, Assemblyman Dan Burling announced a $529,280 Transportation Enhancement Grant to rehabilitate the bridge.

SINGING BRIDGES GO SILENT: The last of the "Singing Bridges" on Route 305 about four miles south of Belfast was silenced by a slab of concrete in September 2002. Originally, there were three spans in close proximity that had steel mesh decks. A vehicle's tires produced a distinctly different hum over each surface, giving rise to the name "Singing Bridges." The bridges crossed over Black Creek and roadbeds of the former Erie and Pennsylvania Railroads.

ALTON SYLOR MEMORIAL BRIDGE: On June 25, 2003, the eyes of the "bridge engineering world" were focused on Angelica. Dedicated to the late Alton Sylor, a former county legislator and chair of the Public Works Committee, the bridge over Joncy Gorge is the largest clearspan timber arch bridge in the nation. It is 274 feet long and located on County Road 16 on the west side of the village.

YORKS CORNERS BRIDGE: Now spanning the Genesee River on County Road 29 is a recycled bridge from the Town of Hume. Department of Public Works Superintendent David Roeske conceived the idea of reusing the 140-foot-long beams that once crossed the defunct Erie River Line Railroad. When the bridge was opened with a ribbon-cutting ceremony on September 23, 2003, Assemblywoman Cathy Young commended Dave Roeske and the Board of Legislators for, "Setting the trends here that we have to look to across the state in the future."

WELLSVILLE'S WEST STATE BRIDGE: On March 9, 2005, the Wellsville Town Board unanimously passed a resolution to dedicate the new (2003) West State Street Bridge in honor of William C. Hennessey, past New York State Department of Transportation Commissioner. This Scio native spent thirty-six years with the DOT, starting as a surveyor's "chainman" and rising to commissioner. Along the way, he headed the State's response to Hurricane Agnes in 1972 and the Governor's Task Force on Love Canal in 1978. (*Editors' Note: A decision was later made to honor Mr. Hennessey by naming Route 19 from Island Park in Wellsville to Scio the William C. Hennessey Memorial Highway.*)

NYS Route 17 Becomes Interstate 86

The Allegany County Board of Supervisors approved by a vote of 21-4 the State's proposed Southern Tier Expressway route on February 22, 1960. This marked the beginning of one of the longest construction periods in Allegany County's history. The initial proposed route of the expressway would parallel then Route 17, now mostly Route 417. Opposition arose and the engineers selected an alternate route that is primarily north of old Route 17 west of Corning to Olean.

Expressway work was started in the county at Cuba in the spring of 1970, progressing east to Friendship. The S. J. Groves Company won the bid for this section at $7,028,841.90 with the total estimated cost in the county at $57,100,000. On September 19, 1974, the Cuba to Friendship section was opened and Friendship to Belvidere section opened on November 1, 1974. Lieutenant Governor Mary Anne Krupsak presided when the Belvidere to Angelica section was opened January 30, 1975. The last section completed in the county was from West Almond to Almond. This was done quietly without fanfare.

In 1997, Samara Barend, an intern working in Senator Daniel Ptrick Moynihan's office, first suggested making the Southern Tier Expressway an Interstate Highway. County Legislator Sue Myers from Friendship "picked up the ball and ran with it," by organizing a local task force. Working with state and federal representatives, Myers efforts paid off handsomely on December 3, 1999, when the road officially became Interstate 86.

The ribbon-cutting ceremony took place on the westbound entry ramp of the Belvidere interchange. Featured speaker was Lieutenant Governor Mary Donohue. Several representatives spoke including State Senator Pat McGee, who, when paying tribute to Legislator Myers, said: "When I hear I-86, I hear Sue Myers." Assemblywoman Cathy Young summed up the rationale for making the road an interstate. She said: "The dream of putting the Southern Tier literally and figuratively on the map by designating Route 17 as I-86 has been realized thanks to the united local commitment. This project is a roadway to increased economic stability and growth in our area by strengthening our transportation infrastructure. It will also showcase the scenic beauty of our Southern Tier and will give tourism a terrific boost."

Opposite page: Ribbon-cutting of Friendship to Belvidere section on November 1, 1974. Left to right are Department of Transportation Resident Engineer Leonard Ladage, Cooperative Extension Agent Kathe Brown, Department of Transportation Regional Director Lewis Hallenbeck, Assemblyman James Emery, and County Legislator Robert McNinch

Top: Paving westbound lane near Angelica using portable concrete batch plant.

Bottom: Dedication speakers for the designation of Route 17 to I-86 on December 3, 1999. Left to right are Assemblywoman Cathy Young, Lieutenant Governor Mary Donohue, Department of Transportation Commissioner Joe Boardman, Senator Pat McGee speaking, Assemblyman Dan Burling, unidentified, unidentified, unidentified, Samara Barend, and Congressman Amo Houghton.

Top: Ribbon-cutting: Left to right are Samara Barend, unidentified, Assemblyman Dan Burling, Assemblywoman Cathy Young, Lieutenant Governor Mary Donohue, Congressman Amo Houghton, unidentified, Department of Transportation Commissioner Joe Boardman, and Department of Transportation Regional Director Peter White.

Middle: Unveiling the new I-86 sign: Left to right are Assemblyman Dan Burling, Congressman Amo Houghton, Lieutenant Governor Mary Donohue, Assemblywoman Cathy Young, unidentified, unidentified, and Samara Barend.

Bottom: Theda Clark from Fillmore first suggested the idea of honoring Allegany County veterans in this manner. Her late husband Lloyd and his brother Alton Sylor served in World War II. Senaor Pat McGee is at the left end of the sign.

The Wellsville Airport

Aviation in the county as we know it today started in 1929 when J. Farnum Brown and George Harris brought the first plane here, landing in a field just northeast of the railroad crossing north of Scio. It was a standard biplane with a Glenn Curtiss OX5 motor and a top speed of ninety miles per hour. Paul McQueen joined them and the Wellsville Flying Club was organized. However, the first plane to fly over the county was piloted by Calbraith P. Rogers on September 24, 1911. By a prearranged plan, a fire alarm was sounded to notify the people of Wellsville of this anticipated spectacle. Within a few minutes after the alarm was sounded, many roofs, telephone poles, bridges, and nearby hills were dotted with residents anxiously awaiting the auspicious approach of the plane. There were possibly five thousand pairs of eyes scanning the eastern horizon for the first glimpse of the "bird man." Using the westbound Erie Railroad tracks as his landmark, Rogers passed the pump station of Elm Valley, which sounded its whistle as an alarm. Within a few minutes at 11:07 a.m., the flying machine was spotted near Wellsville becoming a thrilling, lifelong memory for the many witnesses.

The first airfield operator and flight instructor was Francis "Stretch" Kane. He was born in 1912 and died in his home on Dry Brook Road in Scio on September 30, 1987, at age seventy-five. His influence in aviation education spanned many decades with one of his students being M. J. "Mote" Tarantine.

In 1940, Wellsville purchased the Crowner farm on the village's west side for $10,000.00. They

Current Wellsville Airport, Tarantine Field

built a north-south runway of 2,400 feet and an east-west runway of 2,200 feet. With Mr. Tarantine serving in the Army Air Corps in World War II, little progress was made in finishing the airport. It opened in 1946 with a sod field.

Mrs. Dot Tarantine at original control tower at first Wellsville Airport

Opposite page: Local pilot George Harris Sr. signed this souvenir postal cover.

In the 1950s, major industries in Allegany County campaigned for a larger facility to better serve their expanding needs. The existing runways were inadequate to meet their requirements of larger and faster aircraft. As a result, the Town Board asked for and received voter approval of a $30,000 bond issue, authorized in a referendum August 7, 1962. That bond issue was the financial basis of the "do-it-yourself" runway that a contractor had estimated at a cost of $72,500. With the cooperation of twelve neighboring towns, equipment was loaned and this joint effort resulted in the airport's size increase to 27 acres, making room for a 3,700 black topped landing strip, 75 feet wide with 50-foot sod aprons. This new runway was officially opened on October 7, 1963, with a ribbon-cutting ceremony. Landing lights were soon added. The first jet aircraft landed on Friday, April 28, 1967. It was a Jet Commander flown by Robert Merriam on a demonstration flight from Oklahoma where the plane was manufactured.

A decision was made to relocate the airport following New York State Department of Transportation survey of 1967, which upheld the local contention that the present field had become "outmoded, outdated and inadequate." The relocation expansion had an attached price of $685,000. The new site at 2,400 feet of elevation is one of the highest points around. The heart of the airport was the 4,300-by-75-foot paved, main runway. The distinct advantage of the longer runway is the ability to land larger and faster jet airplanes to better serve the changing needs of business. These new planes rely heavily on the full instrumentation capabilities the new field offers.

The new airport was operational as of November 1970 while formal ceremonies on June 20, 1971, marked the official opening of the Wellsville Municipal Airport. An integral part of the ceremony was the naming of the airfield after M. J. Tarantine, the "Father Of Wellsville Aviation." Among many dignitaries participating in the dedication ceremony were Assemblyman Frank Walkley, Mayor Robert Gardner, Town Supervisor Newton Phillips, and County Legislators David Haskins and Charles Shine. Acknowledged at the ceremony was Town Board member Karl Vossler, whose terms in office spanned both the beginning of the original airport and the signing of the contract for the new one. The success of this project was due primarily to efforts expended by leaders of local industries: namely Air Preheater, Worthington, and Joyce Pipeline, working together with the Village and Town Boards of Wellsville.

Mr. Tarantine was manager from 1945 until he retired, effective December 31,1974. Gary Barnes became manager on January 1, 1975. In 1984–85 the runway was lengthened from 4,300 feet to 5,300 feet. In 1995–96, it was widened from 75 feet to 100 feet. These improvements at the new airport allowed larger planes to land safely, enabling the first jet to do so in the early 1990s.

Under the management of Mr. Barnes, the Wellsville Flying Service leases the airport from the Town of Wellsville. The largest single corporate user of the airport today is Adelphia Communications. They currently operate two planes, employ five full-time pilots, three mechanics, and a manager. The facility averages fifteen to twenty thousand operations per year. The Federal Aviation Administration considers an operation to be a take-off or a landing.

Allegany County Transit

This public bus service in the county started in March 2000. In its first two years of operating, the number of riders ranged between twenty-nine and thirty thousand. In 2003, thirty-four thousand rode the buses. The company divided Allegany County into two zones—east and west of the Genesee River, with a number of different routes throughout. Connections can be made with public transit in adjoining counties. Principle funding for the transit company comes from federal and state subsidies.

chapter 9

BUSINESS AND INDUSTRY

"Pardon My Boarding House Reach"

The traveling public has relied on a multitude of facilities for accommodations, food, and spirits. In the early 1800s inns were commonplace with transportation primarily via stagecoach or horseback. Hotels with three or more floors prospered in the Allegany County area in the mid- to late 1800s; these were located in almost every community. Boarding houses evolved to accommodate the gainfully employed who didn't own their own homes, yet desired associated amenities. They paid their room and board to the proprietor and received family-style meals.

HOTELS: With improved forms of transportation and population increase came larger hotels. One of the most well-known facilities was the Fassett House on North Main Street in Wellsville. (See chapter 13.) The Brunswick Hotel on North Main Street in Wellsville was in operation for many years and today houses several small businesses. Another famous Wellsville Hotel was Pickup's that burned in 1961.

Large hotels also existed in Fillmore, Cuba, Friendship, and Bolivar. The old hotel in Oramel, Town of Caneadea, reopened in May of 1926 to provide rooms and meals for some of the men constructing the Caneadea Gorge Power Dam. Another well-known hotel was the Belmont Hotel built in 1880. (For many years the County Board of Supervisors met here. See Chapter 16.) Today it houses the Fountain Arts Center, Inc., operated by owner Wendy Skinner.

MOTELS: The popularity of the automobile and improved highways fostered the growth of "motor hotels" commonly called motels. At first, motels were fairly small consisting of only one floor. A major change took place in motel operations when the first chain motel opened in the county; this being the Microtel in Wellsville, opening in May of 2002. The Wellsville Motel changed its name when it joined the Best Value Inn chain in October 2001. Many motels are located throughout the county today.

◀ *Note the "Hoover and Curtis" campaign sign for the future president and vice-president (Herbert Hoover and Charles Curtis) over Andover's Main Street in the summer of 1928. The sign at right beckons to tourists.*

Above: The Riverview Motel in Belmont, seen here in 1959, is now part of Allegany County Community Opportunities and Rural Development, Inc. (ACCORD).

Opposite page, top: Fox's Inn Restaurant, between Belvidere and Friendship, 1937. (Photo courtesy of Bette Stockman)

Opposite page, bottom: The Cow Palace in Whitesville boasted that it was "The only place of its kind in the world! Where Lady Holsteins are bought and sold in royal surroundings and you may dine graciously. . . ."

"B AND B'S": The latest trend for the traveling public is the Bed and Breakfast concept, commonly called "B and B's." Before this name became popular, they were called "guest houses" but breakfast usually wasn't included. Many "B and B's" can be found in all parts of the county today.

RESTAURANTS: The restaurant industry in Allegany County certainly has "tasted" its share of change. It is not practical to list all the restaurants that have opened and closed in the last century. However, four deserve recognition; of these, three are still in business while the fourth has been "put out to pasture."

Texas Hot in Wellsville first opened its doors in 1921, started by George Raptis and James Rigas. It is still owned and operated by direct descendents of the founders. The Texas Hot was named for what has become its most famous product and has thrived since it opened.

Maple Tree Inn in the Town of Allen is more commonly called "The Pancake House." This family owned and seasonally operated restaurant opened in 1963, featuring buckwheat pancakes. The restaurant was started by Virginia and Ron Cartwright and is operated by their children today.

Located in the hamlet of Whitesville, The Cow Palace Restaurant was opened in 1961 by D. H. and Peg Rumsey. It would be an understatement to say the restaurant was "unusual." People dined in the "Baron's Banquette" room while the cows did the same on the other side of the plate-glass partition. Mr. Rumsey was forced to give up the cows and eventually the restaurant changed hands and was operating as late as 1968. The building was torn down in 1977 with the site on Main Street now occupied by the Independence Volunteer Ambulance Company.

Travel Port Express—"the Truckstop," restaurant in Belvidere opened in the mid-1970s operating as the only twenty-four-hour restaurant in the county and is open every day.

Cultural changes in Allegany County brought on by a faster, more mobile society, inevitably led to the arrival of the "fast food" industry in the county. The first of these being McDonald's in Wellsville, opening in November 1977. The other McDonald's in the county opened in Cuba adjacent to the Route 17 interchange in the summer of 1991, capitalizing on the increased traffic on the now I-86.

Significant Industries of the Past, Gone but Not Forgotten

ACME ELECTRIC: In 1936, a group of Cuba businessmen heard about an Ohio firm's desire to expand. Members of this group not only telephoned Ohio, but also made an appointment to meet with company representatives the next day in Cleveland. They quickly prepared a prospectus and entrained for Cleveland that night. The men returned with great enthusiasm and were able to generate enough interest from Cuba residents to spearhead a fundraising campaign through the Chamber of Commerce. This campaign raised $53,725 in pledges for the Acme Building Fund. The significance of this is further appreciated by the fact it was done during the depths of the Great Depression. A building was constructed and a community ox roast was held on July 4, 1937. The next day, with about forty employees, operations officially began. Peak employment reached four hundred. Later becoming an electronics firm, it was sold in 2003 to Tracewell Systems of Ohio. What goes around, comes around.

CELADON TERRA COTTA TILE COMPANY: In the 1880s, it was learned that clay found in the area around Alfred could be used to make terra-cotta products, in particular, bricks and roof tiles. A large manufacturing plant was soon built on the site occupied today by Alfred University's McLane Center. The plant primarily manufactured the distinctive red tiles for roofs that were shipped by rail all over the country. Many buildings in Allegany County, particularly in the Alfred area, sport these roofs today. Celadon also manufactured ornamental tiles for home exteriors consisting of bas-relief, heads, fruit, and geometric designs.

The small building serving as the company's office, known as The Terra Cotta, today is the museum for the Alfred Historical Society located on North Main Street. Its exterior walls are adorned with examples of their distinctive and decorative tiles. The building served as the company's catalog for prospective buyers.

Celadon Terra Cotta Corporate Office building, shown here being moved, is now a museum owned and operated by the Alfred Historical Society.

With the exception of the office, the original plant burned in 1909, ending the company's existence. In the few years the company prospered, it was partially responsible for the forming of the New York School of Clayworking in Alfred that has evolved into the New York State College of Ceramics at Alfred University. This college is regarded worldwide as a leading institution in glass science and ceramic engineering.

CUBA CHEESE: Cuba's fame for cheese dates back to 1870. Its zenith came in the early 1900s when cheddar dealers met in a building at Cuba's four corners on a weekly basis to establish the worldwide price. Today, those companies have been merged and consolidated into Empire Cheese, Inc., effective in 1993. It numbers among their primary customers several major cheese companies known around the world.

The Cuba Cheese Shoppe today is appropriately located in an old 1886 cheese warehouse, lending the ambiance of days gone by. They carry a variety of cheeses and condiments.

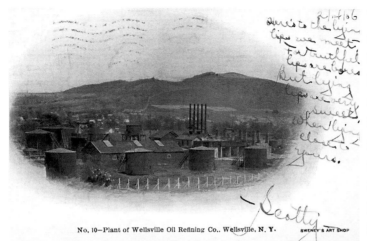

No, 10—Plant of Wellsville Oil Refining Co.. Wellsville. N. Y.

The Cuba Cheese Museum is the newest museum in Allegany County having held a preview opening on November 27, 2004. Its format is to document the history of cheesemaking and ancillary businesses in the region. The Cheese Museum was founded by Velma Moses, Nico Van Zwanenberg, Ellsworth Swift, Betty Edwards, Jack and Mary Nease, Ellen Scott, Judy Zayac, Bonnie Blair, and Don and Carol Donovan who also serve as curators.

JOYCE PIPELINE CORPORATION: What began as a business with one man and a backhoe in 1948 grew into one of the largest pipeline installation companies in the country. In 1967, the company employed one thousand in various states during the peak construction season and had 521 pieces of heavy equipment and trucks. The man who did this is James Joyce. Brother Charles joined the firm in 1950 and built his reputation as a top field superintendent. Brother William (Don) joined the company

Top: This postcard contains a rather risqué message for the time it was sent to a young lady on Valentine's Day, 1906.

Bottom: This Wellsville Oil Refinery Office Building was located near the refinery on South Brooklyn Avenue about 1901.

in 1955 as superintendent of distribution work. James also formed the Joyce Western Corporation that performed numerous public works projects in the Flood of 1972, Hurricane Agnes recovery programs. The company ceased operations in the 1980s.

SINCLAIR REFINERY: The best-known "ghost of industries past" is the Sinclair Refinery that was located on South Brooklyn Avenue in Wellsville. The "oil boom days" in the region started in 1882, lasting some twelve years or so. In November 1901, the Wellsville Refining Company constructed the first refinery. As the oil has a paraffin base, a wax plant was built in 1905. By 1918, the Union Petroleum Company owned the stock and in 1919 sold its operation to Sinclair Refining. By this time, crude oil obtained by primary recovery methods was nearly exhausted. Starting in the early 1920s, secondary recovery by "flooding" wells with water once again stabilized oil production and the refinery business locally. Consequently, the plant was enlarged in 1931 with a reputed capacity of ten thousand barrels of crude per day and has been described as being a $10 million facility. (For the demise of the Sinclair Refinery, refer to Chapter 13.)

However, the "spectre" of Sinclair would literally surface later in Wellsville's history. For whatever reason, tons of toxic chemicals were buried on refinery grounds. On March 28, 1985, New York State Department of Environmental Conservation (NYS-DEC) Commissioner Henry Williams, when addressing those attending a Southern Tier West Regional Planning Board dinner in Cuba said: "The Sinclair Refinery site is one of the worst toxic waste sites in New York." Williams further noted, "we know the

The Sinclair stack comes down with a bang and a boom on October 31, 1993.

chemicals are there, but this countryside is beautiful and has tremendous potential. The key is identifying problems instead of pretending they are not there." The site was declared the most toxic in the state and the sixth worst in the nation after being placed on the Federal Superfund Cleanup list in 1982. Initial remediation costs at the entire site, about ninety acres, were placed at about $9 million.

In 1969, the Atlantic-Richfield Corportion (ARCO) acquired the assets of the Sinclair Oil Corporation. In January 1987, ARCO agreed to pay New York State $6 million for cleanup. In July 1987, the federal Environmental Protection Agency (EPA) awarded a $1 million grant from its Superfund to the NYS-DEC for remediation work. By September 1987, a total of $13.7 million had been allocated for the cleanup and remediation work. Some of this work included rechanneling the Genesee River to divert it from the ten-acre primary chemical burial site. Plans were also drawn up to place a temporary cap on the landfill site and a permanent cap after the official investigation and cleanup was completed. The site cleanup project was completed in 1994.

The EPA issued a report in fall 2002 that stated: "since 1997, the site has experienced an intermittent migration of light, nonaqueous phase liquid into the Genesee River from various seep points." This issue was addressed by the placement of oil booms and absorbent pads with ARCO being told to develop an alternate remedy. In October 2004, ARCO representatives met with Upper Genesee Chapter of Trout Unlimited members and announced they would initiate additional remediation plans in 2007.

The destruction of a monument to Wellsville's industrial past started with a puff of smoke and ended with a thunderous roar on Saturday, October 31, 1993. The last smokestack of the former Sinclair Refinery took just six seconds to succumb to the effects of an exploding nitro charge and gravity. With the demolition just a month earlier of the largest remaining building, the powerhouse, the smokestack stood alone, bearing mute testimony to an industry that, for decades, had employed several thousand Allegany County residents.

At 9:05 a.m., the final warning siren blew and Janet Coppini, secretary in ARCO's Wellsville office, was given the distinction of "pushing the plunger," actually a button, initiating sixteen individual explosions, microseconds apart, from fourteen pounds of nitroglycerin strategically placed at one side of the stack at its base. She was a safe distance away—behind a building. Doug Loizeaux, project manager for Controlled Demolitions, Inc., described the event saying: "Our strategy is to blow a big smile on one side and notch it like you would fell a tree." The stack fell safely, exactly where they had planned. After cleaning up, Doug and his crew took their fee of $30,000 and walked away contented.

"The Business of America is Business."

—President Calvin Coolidge

According to John Foels, the county's economic development director, there are over seven hundred businesses that call Allegany County home. Due to such a large number, we can only write about large or significant ones known throughout the county and/or those which have had major influence in the lives of county residents.

ADELPHIA COMMUNICATIONS: Wellsville native John Rigas moved to Coudersport, Pennsylvania, in the early 1950s with little more than a few hundred dollars in his pocket. He started a new business, virtually unknown in those days—that of a television cable franchise. With a little bit of luck, a great deal of hard work and business savvy, he parlayed his hundreds into millions. The company grew to become the nation's fifth largest cable television operator with about 5.5 million customers.

However, the winds of fortune became ill winds when founder John Rigas and sons Michael, Timothy, and James were forced to relinquish control of the company over alleged illegal accounting practices. In July of 2002, John, Michael, and Timothy and other company officials were charged with wrongdoing by the Securities and Exchange Commission and subsequently arrested. While John and son Timothy were later convicted for their roles in an accounting fraud at Adelphia, Michael's trial ended in a jury-deadlock. Sentencing for John and Timothy is pending as of April 2005, and prosecutors hope to retry Michael Rigas on securities fraud charges.

In March 2003, Adelphia moved its corporate headquarters from Coudersport to Denver, Colorado. With approximately fifteen hundred people working for Adelphia in the Coudersport area and many

The relationship between industry and rail transportation is apparent.

living in Allegany County, concern for the survival of the corporation is great. An additional effect of the massive change in Adelphia was the huge drop in value of company stock with local investors losing thousands of dollars. On April 25, 2005, the Rigas family agreed to forfeit $1.5 billion in assets to Adelphia, who in turn will deposit $715 million in a fund the government will use to compensate investors hurt by the fraud.

AIR PREHEATER COMPANY: An air preheater is a machine designed to utilize heat that would otherwise be lost out the smokestacks of industrial and central power station boilers. In the preheater, this waste heat is captured before it reaches the stack and is transferred to the incoming cold air. The more heat added to this cold combustion air, the greater the savings in fuel that would be required to heat this air in the boiler or furnace.

The Air Preheater Corporation was formed in 1925. Plant No. 1 on South Main Street in Wellsville is its oldest building and is called "Main Street Plant." Two office buildings and a large manufacturing facility are located on Route 417 East. The company's official name is Alstom Power, Inc., Air Preheater Company, and Edward Bysiek serves as president. Wellsville native John Hennessy served as the company's eighth president, retiring in 1986. For additional information see Chapter 8, Conrail section.

DRESSER-RAND ENERGY SYSTEMS: If someone were to listen closely to "old-timers" conversation in much of the county, one would inevitably hear this industry called "Worthington or Turbodyne." And for good reason as these are some of the more recent names for this huge facility. Starting as Moore Steam Turbine in 1916, it was acquired by Worthington Pump and Machinery Corporation in 1936, later became Worthington Turbodyne International, Steam Turbine Division of Turbodyne International and several others. The current name came into existence with the formation of a fifty-fifty joint venture proposed in June 1986 by Dresser Industries and Ingersoll Rand. As of February 2000, Ingersoll Rand acquired full ownership of Dresser-Rand. In August 2004, First Reserve Fund purchased the company.

In the 1960s during the height of "the Cold War," Worthington helped develop a secret submarine that is the only U.S. manned sub capable of diving to some of the deepest parts of the ocean. Engineers and shopworkers in Wellsville designed and manufactured the tiny stainless steel generator that drives the ship.

A new book on the subject called *Dark Waters* was recently released. This is indicative of the highly engineered compressors and turbines Dresser-Rand designs and produces.

EMPIRE CHEESE, INC.: Empire Cheese Company purchased Cuba Cheese in 1993. They manufacture, package and ship provolone and mozzarella cheeses under a variety of labels. (See Chapter 2 for additional background information.)

FRIENDSHIP DAIRIES, INC.: In 1926, John Schanback purchased a lease on the Gilt Edge Cheese Factory in the Friendship area, formerly owned by local farmers. He operated it until 1937 producing cottage cheese, American cheese, and butter, whereupon he built a new plant that he ran until 1957. Schanback and his son Martin purchased a farm one mile east of Friendship and built a new, larger facility enabling them to add lines of Grade A milk and sour cream products. They also built a waste-treatment plant to accommodate their needs. Martin serves as president with his son Warren serving as vice-president with corporate offices in the New York City area. Greg Knapp is currently plant manager overseeing an average of 180 employees.

A major percentage of its sales are in the New York City area because it is a kosher plant, meaning it is operated within the constraints of Jewish dietary laws. As a kosher plant, Friendship uses no preservatives in its products. A rabbi from Buffalo makes regular weekly inspections of the plant and lives there during Passover season when all kosher products must be blessed.

NORTHERN LIGHTS CANDLES: Founder Andy Glanzman is proud to say he and his wife Tina started their company on a "candle string" in 1978. Making hand-dipped functional candles in his small workshop at first, he quickly realized the tremendous market potential of whimsical creations like wiz-

Above: Moore Steam Turbine Corporation was a predecessor of Dresser.

Opposite page, left: Kerr Turbine Company, founded in 1901, was located on South Main Street in Wellsville until it was torn down in 1932.

Opposite page, middle: Clark Brothers Machine Shop in Belmont started in 1880.

Opposite page, right: Fire destroyed the Clark Brothers plant in May of 1912. They subsequently relocated to Olean and were purchased by Dresser.

ards, dragons, and myriad other such designs. They established corporate offices and extensive candle-making facilities in Wellsville on Route 417 east. The company purchased the former Ames store that closed in October 2002. During peak season, they employ over four hundred people and have sales in twenty-nine countries.

OTIS EASTERN SERVICE, INC.: The company started as a regional division of Otis Engineering in 1936 in Dallas, Texas. In 1981, Charles H. Joyce and Charles P. Joyce purchased Otis and changed its focus to the construction and rehabilitation of cross-country transmission pipelines. Today the company is one of the leading pipeline contractors in the United States. President is Charles P. Joyce, vice-presidents are Dick Joyce and Tony Deusenbery with Betty Joyce serving as secretary/treasurer. Year-round employees number about fifty while seasonal employment is approximately five hundred.

STEARNS POULTRY: This family enterprise was started in 1937 by John Stearns at the old homestead on Hartsville Hill in the Town of Alfred. It moved to its present location on Route 244 in the

One of two local plants of the
Air Preheater Corporation
serving the power industry.

The 10,000 barrel refinery of
the Sinclair Refining Co.
processing highest quality
lubricants from local crude
oil.

The Worthington Corporation
builds turbines in this plant
for diversified power appli-
cations.

Proud workers pose inside the Clark Brothers Machine Shop in Belmont.

This back cover of a 1955 Wellsville Chamber of Commerce brochure shows Wellsville's major industries.

"heart of Tinkertown" in 1941. The business grew under the leadership of his son and daughter-in-law, Judson and Margaret. The business expanded and in 1951 opened a retail store in Hornell. In 1985, Judson Stearns II took over the business. Today, the name "Stearns BBQ Chicken" is widely known throughout Allegany County.

SOUTHERN TIER CONCRETE PRODUCTS COMPANY: Benjamin H. Palmer Sr. and son Benjamin Jr. started their concrete building block manufacturing business in 1946 in Alfred on the edge of "Tinkertown." In 1959, it became the first automated block plant in New York State. Benjamin Palmer III is president and Charles Jessup is general manager.

The business manufactures a wide variety of concrete building materials and makes deliveries within a ninety-mile radius of Alfred. Their seasonal number of employees peaks around fifteen.

THE L. C. WHITFORD COMPANY, INC.: In 1916 Langford (Ford) C. Whitford founded the L. C. Whitford Company, Inc., in Wellsville. The company grew under the leadership of the founder's son L. Rodman (Rod) Whitford. Presently, third generation L. Chandler (Chan) Whitford serves as president while fourth generation L. Bradley Whitford serves as vice-president.

The company submits bids for road building and other major construction projects primarily in New York, Pennsylvania, and Ohio from their Wellsville headquarters. From a branch office in Atlanta, Georgia, the company also bids on construction projects in that region and surrounding states. Recently

Southern Tier Concrete when it started in 1946 and on its Fiftieth Anniversary in 1996.

it has secured contracts with Norfolk Southern Railroad for bridge construction in nine states, generally in the Mid-Atlantic region.

Current operations include a full-service construction materials division, three concrete plants, a pre-cast/prestressed concrete manufacturing facility and two asphalt plants. Total company year-round employment is approximately 250 with seasonal opportunities for up to eight hundred employees.

L. C. Whitford has left its mark of quality construction on the landscape of Allegany County. Some of these prominent landmarks include: the David A. Howe Memorial Library in Wellsville (1935), the Allegany County Courthouse in Belmont (1937), Jones Memorial Hospital's third floor (1966), and the Riverwalk Plaza in Wellsville (1994).

Gas and Oil Futures

While writing the history of the oil industry in Allegany County is relatively easy, writing about gas and oil futures is impossible for lay people. Therefore, we have taken the liberty of inviting the area's foremost geologist Mr. Arthur M. Van Tyne of Wellsville to submit his thoughts. He has graciously consented and has submitted the following paper.

Oil and Gas In Allegany County 1950–2005

During the last fifty-plus years, Allegany County has dropped from being the largest oil-producing county in New York to one of the lowest. In fact, all of New York's oil production has dropped to an inconse-

Top left: The first successful well "came in" at Richburg on April 17, 1881. This is Richburg as it appeared in the first oil boom days of 1882.

Bottom left: Nitroglycerine magazine in Bolivar, circa 1907

Right: This oil well "came in" at Bolivar thanks to nitroglycerine.

quential level during this interval. Presently, oil is no longer a significant factor in Allegany County economics. On the other hand, the production of natural gas remains a steady and important part of Allegany County's mineral resource income.

Drilling for shallow oil and natural gas in the 1950s amounted to several hundred wells per year and has now declined to a level of only five to fifteen wells per year. Such drilling only occurs when the prices for oil and/or natural gas rise substantially above average and remain there for a few years. In that case, wells are drilled around the edges of the known productive areas where lower levels of production are obtained. Such production would not be economic to drill for if the prices were low. When the prices go down again, drilling stops. Although drilling for shallow oil and gas production in Allegany County is erratic and price dependent, drilling exploratory wells in hopes of finding deeper gas deposits has continued on a fairly regular basis.

In April of 1958, Parsons Brothers, a Pennsylvania coal operator, moved a drilling rig onto the Cook farm in the southern part of the Town of Hume in northern Allegany County. He planned to drill an exploratory well to the Medina sandstone that would be at a depth of about 4,000 feet. The Medina is a good gas producer farther to the west in Cattaraugus County and beyond, but has not been known to be a good producer in Allegany County. He was only able to drill to a depth of 2,895 feet (through the Oriskany Horizon where there was no sandstone) when his drilling equipment became stuck in the hole. After several tries to clear the bit from the hole, he abandoned the well site and moved in a new rig about two hundred feet to the south where he drilled another hole. This was in late 1958. By August 1959, he had reached a depth of 7,337 feet and the well had become the deepest ever drilled in Allegany County. Unfortunately, salt water was encountered at that depth and the flow could not be shut off. It was plugged in June 1960 without obtaining any gas.

In late 1962, the New York State Natural Gas Corporation sited a location for a deep well on the Wolfer farm in the Town of Hume about one and one-half miles to the northeast of the two Cook wells. By the end of January 1963, the well, drilled with a rotary drilling rig, had reached a total depth of 7,560 feet to become the deepest well in Allegany County thus erasing the record of the second Cook well. Gas was not found in the Wolfer Well but it still retains the distinction of being the deepest well in the county.

In May of 1970, Amity Gas Corporation commenced drilling a well on the Vincent Middaugh farm in the Town of Amity. By September of that year, the well had reached a depth of 6,084 feet through the Medina sandstone formation. No gas was encountered and the well was plugged. This well is the deepest down dip Medina penetration in the county.

In early 1970, gas was discovered in the Oriskany sandstone formation from a well on the Maybee farm and also on the Ramsey farm in the Town of Scio. A company called Professional Petroleum Exploration drilled those wells and several others, some dry, to establish the Gordon Brook gas field. When the field was put on production, it responded quite well for a few years but increasing saltwater flows eventually killed production in all but one of the original wells. That well, on the Ramsey farm, continued to produce gas in a declining amount. In the early 1980s, a new company called Vandermark Exploration purchased the field. Under the direction of the author, Vandermark proceeded to drill new wells and extended the limits of the field by finding new areas of production. The last Vandermark wells were drilled in the late 1990s. The field continues to produce gas at a good rate and has become the most successful Oriskany gas field discovered in New York since the 1930s and 1940s.

In 1979, a well was drilled on the north edge of the Houghton College Campus by the New York State Energy Research and Development Authority (NYSERDA) jointly with the United States Department of Energy (US-DOE). The well was part of a drilling program designed to stimulate private industry to drill for Devonian black shale gas reserves. The Houghton well was drilled to a depth of 2,334 feet ending in the Onondaga limestone. The producing formation was the Marcellus black shale that is just

Above: This is a typical oil-field scene when laying new pipe, 1914.

Left: Carpenters posed on the roof of the oil pump station on Pump Station Road in Alma after its February 1915 explosion and fire.

Opposite page: Note their extensive inventory of pipe for the oil industry in this 1951 aerial view of the Bradford Supply Company in Bolivar, now Hahn and Schaffner.

above the Onondaga. This first Houghton College well was successful and produced enough gas to heat three nearby buildings for several years. A second well, drilled about one mile from the first well, produced only a small amount of gas and was later plugged. The first Houghton College well is unique in that it has produced more gas than any of the other fifteen wells drilled in New York under the NYSERDA–US-DOE program. In fact, reliable information indicates that it has also produced more gas than any of a dozen or so black shale wells drilled by private operators in the 1980s. The Houghton well stands alone as a successful Allegany County Devonian black shale gas producer.

The storage of natural gas in depleted and abandoned subsurface gas reservoirs has, over the years, become a major part of the natural gas industry. By doing this, the natural gas utilities are able to buy gas for a less expensive rate during the summer, and send it to storage. It's available then during the winter to send out on peak, or over peak, demand days during severely cold weather. Allegany County has four such underground storage facilities. A very small, one well field near Richburg called the Gilbert storage has been out-of-service for many years but the three others, all Oriskany sandstone producers, are still active. East Independence was activated for storage in 1972. West Independence and Beech Hill were undergoing preparations for storage from 1979 to 1982 and were put into service after that. These are both large, old gas fields owned by National Fuel Gas in Buffalo and they make Allegany County a leader in the gas storage field business. When the State Line gas field, also now owned by National Fuel Gas, and located just across the Genesee River Valley southwest of Beech Hill, is converted to storage, it will be the largest gas storage field in New York State. The entire Independence, Beech Hill and State Line complex would then be capable of storing over 100 billion cubic feet of gas—a very substantial figure for any gas storage field anywhere.

During the late 1970s and 1980s, some wells owned by Cunningham Natural Gas in the State Line field suddenly began to flow gas heavily. These wells were producing at a low level with substantial salt water and the new higher gas and saltwater production nearly overwhelmed the company's operations. They soon brought in railroad tank cars to handle the brine and had to revamp their sales line to handle the new higher pressures and increased volume of gas. It appears that the storage operation to the northeast at Beech Hill may have dislodged a huge bubble of gas that migrated up-structure to the Cunningham wells. National Fuel Gas, owner of the Beech Hill storage, sued Cunningham and contended that the new gas he was producing was gas they had injected into the Beech Hill storage field. Dye was injected into National Fuel's gas and other measurements were taken but it was never proven that Cunningham's new production came from National Fuel. The matter was finally settled when National Fuel bought out Cunningham. This has become a landmark case showing the highly complex structural nature of some of the rocks under Allegany County. In this case, this complexity hid the source of a very large volume of subsurface gas.

These are some of the more prominent developments that have taken place in the oil and gas industry of Allegany County during the past fifty-five years. Oil is no longer king but there remains a billion barrels of oil in the shallow rocks below Allegany County. Some form of Tertiary Recovery may yet be used to recover much of that oil. If so, then the county could experience another cycle of prosperity like the previous one. Little is known about the potential for deep natural gas deposits here and these too, may provide a future boom in drilling and discovery.

Contributed by Arthur M. Van Tyne,
Formerly Senior Geologist in-charge,
Oil and Gas Research Office
New York State Geological Survey.
Currently, Consulting Petroleum Geologist

chapter 10

COMMUNICATION–BACK FENCE TO CHAT ROOMS

The ability to adequately communicate with each other has always been of paramount importance. For centuries, simple face-to-face conversation with friends over the back fence sufficed. This would soon change in the twentieth century. No longer content to wait days to receive a letter, people today practically demand electronic replies in seconds. Conversations and opinions are now shared electronically via e-mail, chat rooms, and instant messaging. This evolution of communication is an intriguing story.

RURAL FREE DELIVERY: Early U.S. Post Office Department mail routes were established in Western New York by 1810, with mail being delivered by horse and rider. Delivery was once or twice a week and rather undependable. During the nineteenth century and some of the first half of the twentieth century, most small post offices were located in a general store with the storekeeper also serving as postmaster. It was convenient for getting mail if you lived near the store, but people in the rural areas were forced to make trips to "town" in order to receive mail. The Grange, a significant organization, took up the cause of mail delivery to rural areas. They petitioned Congress who authorized the Post Office Department to initiate Rural Free Delivery (RFD) in 1896. Benefits of RFD were almost immediate: roads were improved to accommodate carriers and the rural folk received mail the same day as their city brethren. The first RFD route in the county was out of Fillmore and started delivery in May of 1901. Dozens more soon followed.

A total of 122 different post offices have served the needs of county residents and of these, 29 are open today. The combination of RFD, improved roads, and better transportation caused many small post offices to become obsolete and they were closed.

By the mid-1890s, much of America's merchandising was handled by two competing giants: Sears and Roebuck and Montgomery Ward. Sears and Roebuck soon gained the advantage by sending mail-order catalogs to every home in America. The change from traditional self-sufficiency to the availability of consumer ready products was at hand and in their mailbox. The cliché of "everything from soup to nuts" certainly applies here. The Sears and Roebuck catalogs offered every house and farm need imaginable, even including houses and barns.

◀ *RFD and parcel post delivery wagon in Almond, circa 1910*

"EXTRA, EXTRA, READ ALL ABOUT IT!" NEWSPAPERS IN ALLEGANY COUNTY: The oldest known copy of a newspaper published in Allegany County was called *The Democratic Sentinel*. The only known issue was published in 1824 in Angelica and is in the hands of a private collector. Angelica served as the county seat from 1806 until 1859, hence, many different short-lived newspapers were published there. The popularity of weekly and monthly local publications grew and reached its apex in the first few decades of the twentieth century. The prominent weekly newspapers of the county included: *Alfred Sun* (still in print), *Andover News*, *Angelica Advocate*, *Belfast Blaze*, *Belmont*

This page: Belvidere Post Office and business block, 1911

Opposite page top: Birdsall Hotel and Post Office, 1910

Opposite page bottom: Little Genesse Post Office and business block, 1910

Dispatch, *Bolivar Breeze*, *Canaseraga Times*, *Cuba Patriot* (still in print), *Friendship Register*, *Northern Allegany County Observer* (Fillmore), *Rushford Spectator*, *Allegany County Democrat* (Wellsville), and *Whitesville News*. Most issues of these papers are on microfilm in various locations in the area. The only daily newspaper published in the county today is the *Wellsville Daily Reporter*. Its banner proudly proclaims: "Serving Allegany County and Northern Pa. Since 1880."

For the most part, local newspapers relied entirely on local merchants for advertising revenue. This changed in the 1950s and 1960s when large, chain grocery stores opened. Consequently, "mom and pop" operations closed their doors. In the mid-1960s, the *Belmont Dispatch* acquired the weeklies from Angelica and Friendship. They finally succumbed and ran their final issue on December 22, 1966. The front-page headline simply said "Eulogy" and was written by Miss Grace Marriner. Her opening paragraph stated: "Something very precious is passing from our midst with this, the final edition of the *Dispatch*. For several generations it has been the mirror of the scenes in life's drama as enacted in our community and its environs. How eagerly we have welcomed its arrival and how thoughtlessly we have taken it for granted." Later she wrote: "Powerful radio, television, and a syndicated press are not only sources of pleasure and information but seeming necessities of modern life." Still further she wrote: "Clifford and Rosemary Grastorf have fought courageously, even by trying to survive by a merger with two other papers and in the face of appalling rise in expenses. This last is undoubtedly due to the upset of our American way of life by too much participation in foreign affairs to the neglect of our own and to the fruitless and expensive wars which we have been waging off and on (mostly on) for the past fifty years."

TELEPHONES: Primitive telephone service was available in Allegany County as early as 1880, having benefited from being on a "through line" in Wellsville, running from Erie, Pennsylvania to Binghamton. In 1889 a line was built from Wellsville to the county home in Angelica with a toll station installed in the Charles Hotel on Park Circle. Various companies became involved in telephone service over the succeeding years with mergers commonplace.

By the 1930s the majority of the county had received telephone service. Of course "service" in those days consisted of party lines with each subscriber having a different ringing pattern. Inevitably, others would pick up their receivers and listen in, hoping to hear the latest "local news."

Charles Ricker, a retired county treasurer, was also an early installer of telephones. In the 1940 publication titled *The Historic Annals of Southwestern New York*, Mr. Ricker wrote about installing the first telephones in homes. He said: "I never installed a telephone in a farmhouse that I didn't receive a thrill at the thought that I had brought this house into connection with most of the neighbors, with the doctor, the railroad station, the village stores and the world; that I had done away with the feeling of isolation and loneliness so often associated with farm life, and had conferred a blessing upon the house. I have seen tears stream down a woman's face the first time she used the new 'phone."

Belfast telephone linemen, circa 1910

Eighty-six original Area Codes were assigned to North America in 1947. All of Western New York was 716 while Central New York was 315. A few years later, lines were redrawn adding the Area Code 607 designation for the eastern fifth of the county. With the advent of fax machines, computers, and cell phones starting in the 1980s, the need for another Area Code became apparent. With the metropolitan areas of Buffalo and Rochester both in Area Code 716, neither region wanted to be reassigned to the new Area Code. Changing telephone numbers would be a costly and lengthy procedure feared by business entities. After a year of lengthy, oft-heated debate, it was decided the greater Rochester area would become part of the new 585 Area Code while greater Buffalo would remain in 716. Most of Allegany County would become part of the new 585 Area Code, except for the area already in 607. An eighteen-month phase-in period culminated with the switch-over to 585 being completed in the spring of 2002.

The last places in Allegany County to have operators and manual switchboards were Wellsville, Bolivar, Belfast, and Cuba. The lights on the Wellsville switchboard went out permanently at 2:01 a.m. on June 18, 1966. The last call they handled was from the New York State Police who made this call from their zone headquarters on the Bolivar Road. They expressed their appreciation for the assistance and cooperation they had received from the operators over the years. These manually operated switchboards were the last in operation to be replaced by the New York Telephone Company. Telephone users in the Wellsville area went directly from operator-assisted calls to direct dial long distance and touch-tone 'phones without several intermittent system improvements. On every call, no longer did the user have to wait and then hear a distinctive voice say: "Operator, Number Please!"

CELL PHONES AND TOWERS: Several large, skeletal steel communication towers began to grace the landscapes in Allegany County in the early 1960s. One of the first in the region was an American

Telegraph and Telephone microwave relay tower on Moland Hill Road in Alfred. In July of 1965, a similar tower was erected on Alma Hill, the highest elevation point in the county.

The widespread use of cell phones, starting in the early 1990s necessitated the construction of strategically placed cell towers throughout the county. Due to the hilly terrain, there are still some "pockets" where cell phones are not operable. Some towers are very conspicuous due to their location along heavily traveled New York State Route 17, now Interstate 86. Cell phone technology dictates that the placement of these towers be line-of-sight and about five miles apart. These six towers, erected in May and June 1994, are clearly visible as you travel on I-86 through the county.

WLSV-790 AM RADIO: Using call letters as an abbreviation of Wellsville, the first commercial AM radio station in the county signed on the air in October of 1955. The original owners were the Bromley, Satterwhite, and Erickson families of Bradford, Pennsylvania. Shortly after, Joseph and Roberta Mumma of Wellsville became partners. The Mummas had been operating the Fassett House since 1945. Roberta Mumma was a very well-known voice to listeners as she hosted a popular show called "Items of Interest," whose format was the publicity of upcoming social events, meetings, and various activities in the area.

The station's first broadcast studios were located in what later became Piscitelli's Barber Shop on the north side of the Fassett House Hotel on Main Street in Wellsville. In the 1960s, the station relocated across the street above Ludden's Shoe Store. In June of 1983, Buzz and Karen Erickson of Belmont purchased the business. They soon moved broadcast facilities to the second floor above the former Key Bank

Andover Telephone Company switchboard in September 1909

Not all "telephone numbers" were numbers in the 1940s. The number of the Sunrise Inn, located at the north end of Cuba Lake, was 5-F-11.

and drive-thru office on Park Avenue.

The critical role of radio in our lives became very apparent during the Flood of 1972 when announcers Bill Jones and Rod Biehler stayed on the air non-stop for five days. This was made possible by a portable generator from McCullough Mighty Light.

Presently the station is owned by Robert Mangels who took over on September 1, 1998. Its original broadcast tower located in Stannards is still in use. The station's format is country and western music. Today it is affiliated with sister station WJQZ-FM with their offices located at 82 Railroad Avenue, Wellsville.

WJQZ 103.5 FM RADIO: The first commercial FM radio station in Allegany County, WJQZ, signed on the air February 3, 1986. This station was owned and started by Scenic Sounds, Inc., a corporation formed in 1985. It was assigned a frequency of 93.5 megahertz. Officers of the corporation included G. Robert Weigand, president; Terry Swift, vice president; Jacqueline Weigand, secretary; and Michael T. Baldwin, news director.

From its studio at 82 Railroad Avenue, Wellsville, it broadcasts an adult-contemporary music format, emphasizing the then-new compact disc medium. The station rented space on a commercial tower on Madison Hill for its antenna and transmitter. Louis Mason of Randolph, also a member of the corporation, constructed a building to house the equipment. The station has changed hands and format several times in the intervening years. It has also changed its frequency to 103.5 FM and moved its antenna site to Alma Hill. Their format today is "golden oldies."

WZKZ-101.9 FM RADIO: The sound of a new radio station was heard in the twin-tier region of New York and Pennsylvania when KZ-102 signed on the air in late February 1999. Their format is contemporary country music. The station is owned by Pembroke Pines Media Group, which is owned by Robert J. Pfuntner of Elmira.

KZ-102 broadcasts at the assigned frequency of 101.9 megahertz with five thousand watts of power. Their broadcast tower is located on Pingrey Hill, Town of Andover, utilizing a five-hundred-foot antenna. The station offers live local news in the morning, at noon and in the afternoon. The station's business and production office is located at 3012 East Side Avenue, Wellsville.

Many radio stations today subscribe to a satellite relay service that insures reliability and stability. While the three area radio stations have live newscasts and "disc jockeys" in addition to special live remote broadcasts, they all utilize the satellite service as well.

"BREAKER! BREAKER! 1-9," HAMS AND CB'ERS: Amateur "ham" radio operators and citizen band "CB" radio operators have proven their worth in times of emergencies and power failures as primary communication relay sources. Ham radio groups have been a stable organization in Allegany County for over seventy years, while today CB radio is primarily used by truckers and other travelers.

"RABBIT EARS WITH CHANNELS 2, 4 AND 7.": The modern miracle of television was available in most parts of Allegany County by the mid-1950s. Your only antenna, resembling rabbit ears, was small and sat on the television. You were also very limited in your choice of channels with most systems only capable of receiving those three channels from Buffalo. Reception usually consisted of a black and white "snowy picture with squiggly lines." Soon large, cumbersome roof antennas sprouted from many roofs somewhat improving reception and the number of available channels. A new technology soon supplanted roof antennas affording another option in television reception. Large, obtrusive dishes were planted in many yards, capable of receiving signals from satellites. Depending

The Hotel Fassett in Wellsville, seen here circa 1960, was the first location of WLSV.

on the availability of a large, open space for best reception, the front yard was the prime location of the satellite dish as its looming presence became a status symbol in rural America.

Small, local cable companies started business in many villages in the county in the late 1950s and early 1960s. For example, Matthew Burzycki of Alfred petitioned the Town Board to erect a television cable serving the area from Alfred to Alfred Station. He was granted the franchise in October of 1961 and later acquired the Almond cable franchise from Albert Palmer. Time Warner Communications purchased Alfred Cable in 2004. Well-known local entrepreneur Gus Rigas started the first Wellsville television cable system. Changing hands several times, the system today is part of Adelphia Communications, Inc. About 1983, Elmar Communications owned by Lance Shaner, established a cable system in Angelica. They are now part of the Time Warner Corporation. Most other communities in the county reflect similar trends in the history of cable television.

COMPUTERS: The old saying, "The world is growing smaller" became a reality with the invention and availability of the computer, thus bringing the world to our doorstep. One of the many major changes they have initiated in our society is the increased number of home-based businesses conducted via computer. Allegany County's rural environment is particularly conducive to this type of business. Virtually unlimited access to information is a mouse click away. In many ways, computers have made it possible for people in rural areas to compete equally with their urban brethren.

Despite all means of communication, Allegany County remains a fractured entity in terms of loyalty to a particular place or media. Allegany County's consumption of news either by radio, television, or newspaper is not limited to one source. No two sections of the county read the same paper, listen to the same local radio station, or watch a common television channel. The only thread uniting the twenty-nine townships in the county is their legal bond with each other.

chapter 11

BANKING, "IN THE PUBLIC INTEREST"

150 Years of Banking in Allegany County

By Erland B. Kailboume
Retired Chairman and CEO Fleet Bank of New York
Current Member New York State Banking Board

I'm most appreciative for having the opportunity and privilege of writing this account of banking in the county of my birth in this year 2005. We often hear the old adage: "What goes around comes around," and that is exactly what has occurred in this segment of Allegany County's financial history.

A search of county historical records reflects that the first chartered bank to operate in the county was a branch of the Brie County Bank that opened in 1855. The First State Bank of Cuba was also chartered that same year.

For nearly a hundred years until 1958, the communities of the county were served with independent banks that prospered and reached seventeen in number by the late 1950s, but as of this year (2005), those institutions have all been merged and banking offices throughout the county presently represent branches of banks headquartered in cities such as Buffalo or Syracuse. Hence we have witnessed this industry come full circle in the last fifteen decades. During the interim, the origination, growth, and function of independently chartered banks provided the capital for the county to grow and prosper as well as develop bankers who have played major roles in the banking environment throughout the Empire State.

As this account of the industry encompasses 150 years, I have chosen to divide the story into three eras—(I) The Early Years 1855–1905, (II) The Development Years 1905–1955, and (III) The Golden Rise and Fall of the County's Great Financial Institutions 1955–2005.

◀ *The Richburg Bank building, seen here circa 1910, stood just north of Richburg School and was razed in 1988.*

(I) The Early Years
1855–1905

As the county historical records reflect, the early settlement of this western region of New York State was driven by the virgin pine forests. As settlers found their way here in the early 1800s, most of the commerce and trade was financed by merchants and privately owned banks which were not subject to state or federal oversight. With the completion of the Erie Railroad and advent of the Civil War and enactment of the National Banking Act in 1864, both state and federally chartered institutions were organized by investors and businessmen to meet the needs of the growing communities throughout the county. The first nationally chartered bank was the First National Bank of Friendship in 1864 (National Charter No. 265).

These newly formed banks are well chronicled in the writings of John P. Herrick, a former resident of Allegany County, in his book *The First 100 Years of Banking in Allegany County* written in 1955. At the time of his account of the first century of banking, he researched the origins of the banks, and in 1955 eight of the seventeen independent banks in the county were operating under national charters. There were nine state-chartered institutions, and four of the seventeen banks in the county had trust powers. The communities that were served by these early institutions were:

Alfred	University Bank of Alfred	September 1, 1894	State Charter
Andover	Andover Bank	January 1, 1894	State Charter
Angelica	First National Bank	November 3, 1864	National Charter
Belfast	First National Bank	January 1, 1882	National Charter
Belmont	Bank of Belmont	June 25, 1888	State Charter
Bolivar	State Bank of Bolivar	May 11, 1882	State Charter
Bolivar	First National Bank	October 2, 1928	National Charter
Canaseraga	Canaseraga State Bank	October 1, 1879	State Charter
Cuba	Cuba National Bank	June 1, 1865	National Charter
Cuba	First National Bank	January 29, 1880	National Charter
		November 4, 1889	State Charter
Friendship	Union National Bank	July 13, 1917	National Charter

(First National Bank—Charter No. 265—and Citizens National Bank of Friendship merged on July 13, 1917.)

Rushford	State Bank of Rushford	December 3, 1921	State Charter
Wellsville	First National Bank	January 2, 1883	National Charter

(Merged into First Trust Company in 1917)

Wellsville	Citizens National Bank	March 12, 1895	National Charter
Whitesville	First National Bank	July 30, 1905	National Charter

On balance for the first fifty years the banks grew slowly and there were only five bank failures: one in Richburg (January 1888) as a result of the boom and bust of the Petrolia Richburg Oil Field discovered in 1881; the National Bank of Angelica in 1886, and three private banks in Wellsville in the early 1880s.

(II) The Development Years
1905–1955

During this period of rural growth and the First and Second World Wars, the banks in Allegany County continued to meet the economic needs of their communities. The rise and fall of the Petrolia Richburg Oil Boom seemed to take the speculators out of the county and the banks were conservatively managed and generally only employed five to fifteen people. They stuck to their knitting and survived the Bank Holiday during the Great Depression in the 1930s, reopening to meet the needs of the World War II era. It was a gentlemen's business and the term "bankers hours" meant a 9:00 to 3:00 job.

Top: The State Bank of Fillmore, 1906

Bottom: The Belfast Bank barely survived the fire of August 6, 1909.

(III) The Golden Rise and Fall of the County's Great Financial Institutions
1955–2005

With the post–World War II era of growth, transportation and industrial activity, the banks in Allegany County commenced to run their activities not only as institutions to facilitate trade and bills of exchange, but as businesses as well. The major population center and industrial hub in the county was the Village of Wellsville. Its growth was fueled by its location on the Erie Railroad, Genesee River, and major East/West Highway—Route 17. Wellsville was also home to two of the most prominent industrial plants in the county, and the bankers of that community capitalized on developing a mini-banking center by the mid-1970s. The competition between the First Trust Company and Citizens National Bank was intense during the three decades of the 1950s, 1960s, and 1970s.

The race for banking supremacy in the county started with the Citizens National Bank when they acquired the Andover National Bank and the University Bank of Alfred in 1956, and the Whitesville National Bank in 1959. This was followed by the acquisition of the State Bank of Bolivar in 1962. The move to bank consolidations for the county was driven by Denton Fuller, a Buffalo banker who became president of the Citizens National Bank in 1941 and left twenty years later to head a bank in Cumberland, Maryland. Mr. Fuller retired to Allegany County after a most illustrious banking career. His frantic pace was sustained by Harold (Monty) Bloss, a most distinguished gentleman who had been president of the Whitesville Bank when he succeeded Fuller as president of the Citizens National Bank in 1961.

First National Bank of Whitesville, 1911

Mr. Bloss was succeeded by Theodore (Ted) McClure who was one of the area's most eloquent speakers and ever in-demand as a toastmaster and most competent banker. Under McClure's tenure, the Citizens National Bank acquired the Cuba National Bank in Cuba, and branched into Cattaraugus County by acquiring the Olean Trust Company.

At the same time, the First Trust Company, headquartered in Wellsville, commenced an acquisition spree of their own by first acquiring the State Bank of Canaseraga in 1957, followed by the Union National Bank of Friendship in 1958. For some thirty years, George Rooth presided as president of the First Trust Company and had worked at the bank for nearly a half century. With the acquisition of the Friendship Bank, First Trust acquired Walter E. Taber, who, with newly named president (1958) career banker Carl Reuning, created a most formidable duo management team that propelled this institution to the forefront of the merger game and became the larger of the two powerful banks headquartered in Wellsville. First Trust acquired the Bank of Angelica in 1959, the First National Bank of Bolivar in 1962, and the First National Bank of Belfast and First National Bank of Cuba in the later part of the 1960s. First Trust was the first to venture into Cattaraugus County with the acquisition of the Union National Bank of Franklinville at the end of the 1960s decade, followed shortly by the First National Bank of Salamanca and the State Bank of Randolph in the early 1970s. First Trust opened a DeNova office in Yorkshire, Olean, and Jamestown in the 1970s to sustain their dominant market presence throughout the western part of the Southern Tier.

As a result of the two Wellsville banks' aggressive acquisition activities, Wellsville became the "money center" of the county by the mid-1970s, as each of these banks had over $100 million in deposits by the close of that decade. The State Bank of Rushford merged with the bank in Arcade, and the two remaining independent banks in Belmont and Fillmore, would eventually be acquired by Citizens and First Trust respectively during this time frame.

During the 1970s, state banking laws were amended to allow statewide branching and as a result, holding companies became prevalent. First Trust Company (First Trust Union Bank after the Franklinville merger) joined Security New York State Corporation, which eventually was acquired by Norstar, then became Fleet Financial and, eventually part of Bank of America, although the Allegany County offices

142

were spun off to the Community Banks Holding Company. The same fate also befell the Citizens National Bank as it became part of Key Corporation. Interestingly enough, two Allegany County natives, Erland "Erkie" Kailbourne and Gary Allen, who started their careers at First Trust and Citizens National Bank respectively, became the CEOs of Fleet Bank and Key Bank, both headquartered in Albany, New York, with vast branch networks throughout New York State. (Fleet's branch network was the largest in numbers of any bank in New York State). These two institutions, with assets in excess of $10 billion each, were the result of bank consolidations throughout New York State including some New York City banks.

Top: Bank of Angelica, 1914

Bottom: First National Bank of Cuba, 1950s

Other prominent bankers who learned their trade in Allegany County went on to play a major role in the state's banking scene during the twentieth century besides Messrs. Allen and Kailbourne, were John F. Thompson and Raymond Ball. Thompson, who at the turn of the century was involved with the Richburg and Bolivar Banks during the Petrolia Oil Field Boom, moved on to the Seaboard National Bank in New York City and later was one of the original organizers and senior officers of Bankers Trust Company. Raymond Ball, who originally was an Allegany County banker and Wellsville native during the mid-1900s, became president of the Lincoln Alliance Bank in Rochester and was also chairman of the University of Rochester and a director of the Eastman Kodak Company.

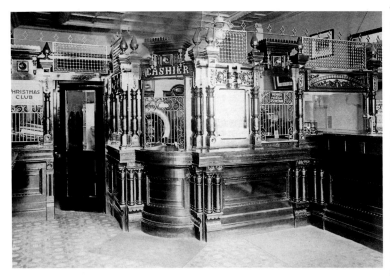

Top: Interior of Citizens National Bank of Wellsville, 1910

Bottom: First National Bank and City Hall in Wellsville, 1915

There were many prominent businessmen and bankers who contributed to the growth of the institutions with which they were affiliated. Unfortunately, all of them cannot be memorialized in this narrative. I would be remiss, however, if I didn't mention some of the individuals or families that contributed to the business of banking during this past century and a half that benefited the county. The Burrows family in Andover played a prominent role in that bank's development, as did the Windsor family with the Canaseraga Bank. Walter Lilly at the Angelica Bank had a long tenure as president, as did Clyde Brown and Hayden Setchel at the two Cuba Banks. Mr. Setchel's son John sustained the family profession. Bill Hogan, president of the State Bank of Bolivar, was considered the "dean of Allegany bankers" with over sixty years of service to that organization. Longevity was a hallmark of that bank's management, as Louis Dunn was also cut from the same mold. Colonel Wellman should also be commended, not only for what his family meant to Friendship, but the Colonel was one of the organizers, officer, and director from the day the bank opened in 1864 to his death in June of 1889.

Probably one of the most influential family names in the county was that of the Willetts family from Belmont. Elmore Willetts Sr. and his son Elmore Jr. reigned over the State Bank of Belmont since that institution's opening on June 25, 1888. The bank was first located in the Belmont Hotel; then it moved to its existing handsome bank structure in 1913. Mr. Willetts was considered one of the wealthiest residents of the county, as evidenced by his mansion in the village and his gift of the Colonial Town Hall to Belmont. Mr. Willetts Sr. was also president of Citizens National Bank of Wellsville from 1897 to 1905. Both he and his son maintained interlocking directorships at the Belmont and Wellsville Banks. Interestingly enough, the Belmont Bank was one of the few in the nation that paid no interest on their deposits for almost a century. (*Editors' Note: The Willetts mansion was originally located on Washington Street in Belmont. About 1909, he offered to fund the building of a new Town and Village Hall if the "village fathers" would change the name of his street to Willetts Avenue. As a result, a Willetts Avenue address in Belmont became one of prestige.)*

Men like Bayard Haskins, Otto and John Walchi, John and Fran Richardson, William Jones who gifted his Wellsville property to the Wellsville Hospital, Thomas Moogan, Ellis Hopkins, George Harris Jr., and E. J. Farnum of Wellsville were great benefactors to their communities. William McKenzie, a longtime director of the State Bank of Belmont was also a prominent New York State assemblyman and chairman of the powerful Ways and Means Committee in the state legislature, during the 1960s. Don O. Cummings, also a prominent assemblyman, was a director of First Trust Union Bank for two decades in the 1960s and 1970s.

There are numerous other individuals who were directors of these banks. The golden era of banking business was the three decades following World War II, when mergers were always being negotiated and competition for deposits and business relationships were intense. This era of growth and competition was prominently on display at the annual Allegany County Bankers picnic from the late 1940s through the 1960s. Over three hundred directors and officers would gather for the annual outing with representatives of all the Buffalo, Rochester, and New York City Banks in attendance as well as principle officers from outside accounting firms and representatives from the Federal Reserve and State Banking Department. Today, as we commence the twenty-first century, we have come full circle as no longer does Allegany County have any independent institutions. The financial needs of the citizens of the county are now provided by branch banks or the internet, all of which support the assessment that "What goes around comes around" and that the only constant in life or business is change itself.

Top: Burrows' Store and Bank in Andover, 1907

Middle: State Bank of Belmont, 1917

Bottom: Willetts Estate is at right on Washington Street (now Willetts Avenue) in Belmont, 1909.

chapter 12

"BELLS, WHISTLES AND SIRENS TOO, VOLUNTEERS TO THE RESCUE"

ALLEGANY COUNTY
1806–2006
BICENTENNIAL

In the best of all worlds, the help of others is still needed upon occasion to assist us in times of personal loss and disaster. When misfortune strikes, members of the fire and ambulance services stand ready to avert potential calamities. These volunteers must undergo extensive training and be willing to make huge personal sacrifices to become accredited. All too often the volunteers are taken for granted, or worse yet, their services aren't even acknowledged by a simple "thank you." Without these volunteers, the well-being of the people and the safeguarding of their property would be severely jeopardized.

Currently, twenty-eight volunteer fire departments and seventeen volunteer ambulance companies serve Allegany County. Some ambulance services are affiliated with a fire department while others are independent. Providing additional assistance upon request is the Medical Transport Service (MTS), a professional ambulance service.

Allegany County Firefighting and Fire Service

The cry of "Fire!" wasn't just limited to battlefields in times of war. For most of the nineteenth century, wooden buildings dotted the landscapes of the county. Fire codes and inspections as we know them today were still decades away. The threat of uncontrolled fire was one of the greatest concerns of the nineteenth-century residents. Once a fire ignited, it most often just burned itself out. Ringing church bells and shouting "Fire!" were the only ways of summoning help. The only means of effectively "fighting" fire was the bucket brigade manned by neighbors and volunteers.

Hand-operated pumps and hose carts pulled by horses or men came into use in the mid- and late 1800s in the county. Perhaps the earliest steamer company in the county was the Genesee Hose Company of the Wellsville Fire Department, organized in June of 1874. Shortly after the Friendship Fire Department was organized in 1881, they purchased a steam pumper named "Daisy." It is the only surviving steam pumper in the county and is being restored to its original operating condition by Tom Cannon and other members of the Friendship Volunteer Fire Department.

◄   *Angelica Hose Company, 1907*

147

148

PETER DUDLEY
Famous Porter of the Hotel Fassett

"Yess Sah, Pleas' Sah"

Meet Me
At
The
Seven
County
Volunteer
Firemen's
Convention
and
Tournament

Annual Inspection Day of Wellsville Fire Department

Wellsville, N. Y., July 14-15 '09

A milestone in local firefighting history was achieved in 1913 when five members of the Genesee Hose Company Running Team from the Wellsville Fire Department set two world records using a handmade hose cart. Competition consisted of pulling a hose cart one hundred yards, laying hose, and getting water on a target. They accomplished this in 27 and 1/5 seconds and 27 and 1/3 seconds respectively. Because of World War I, the running team was abandoned and this friendly competition among fire departments across the country died out. By 1920, most of the firefighting apparatus in the county had become motorized.

For much of the early twentieth century, communication between firefighting units was by telephone. By the early 1950s, most vehicles were equipped with two-way radios. The first of the so-called "fire dispatch centers" was established in the home of Edwin Olmsted on Triana Street in Belmont in 1955. Due to health problems he retired effective July 1, 1963. County Fire Coordinator Robert Burgess of Canaseraga interviewed eight potential replacements and selected George and Melba Mickle from Andover as the new dispatchers. The operating unit in their home on East Greenwood Street sent signals to the base transmitter on Joyce Hill via leased telephones lines. After the passing of her husband in June of 1969, "Mel" assumed sole responsibility, quickly becoming a "legend in her own time." During her tenure, she handled calls for all twenty-nine of the county's fire departments plus several in nearby Pennsylvania communities. Additionally she logged calls for fourteen ambulance squads, the County Rescue Squad in Wellsville, and the Andover Police Department. She also operated the county's mutual aid dispatch system. All fire departments were assigned call letters and numbers by the Federal Communications Commission. With her distinctive gravelly voice, Mel was known and loved by all simply as "Mrs. KED-620." Mel would temporarily relinquish her duties on Sunday afternoons and rare times during the week. A rotating list of substitute dispatchers, including Spud and Jean Glover from Andover, Don and Norilyn Patrick from Belmont, Billy Braun, John Fleischman, Bill Jones and Althea Smith from Wellsville, Don and Linda Bledsoe from Fillmore, Walt and Jean Lang from Alfred, and Larry Dye from Cuba filled in for Mel.

At a meeting of the Allegany County Volunteer Firemen's Association on January 20, 1988, Mel submitted her letter of resignation to Fire Coordinator Keith Barber from Rossburg. She stated she would not renew her contract when it expired in December. Mr. Barber said: "It's a letter I'd hoped I'd never receive." The end of an era was present. Mel Mickle died on November 12, 1997. Firefighting and ambulance vehicles comprised a large portion of her funeral procession in Andover, indicative of the respect and admiration she had earned from all who knew her. The "Voice of KED 620" fell silent forever.

Opposite page top: Firemen's Parade in Belmont, 1911, in front of Belmont's first fire hall located on North Street. The old village jail was located in the back of the building, which was torn down in 2004.

Opposite page bottom: Peter Dudley was a member of McEwen Hose Company and very popular in Wellsville.

This page: Mel Mickle conducting a noon Saturday siren test on December 10, 1988.

In 1988, speculation began as how best to fill Mel's position. One possibility was to hire several people to perform her duties. Technological changes now made 9-1-1 a distinct possibility and the County Board of Legislators opted for this plan. The decision was made to move the entire dispatching operation to the Allegany County Office Building in Belmont. Equipment was purchased and the new center was located on the ground floor in the Fire Coordinator's Office. At midnight, December 31, 1988, Mel Mickle at KED 620 in Andover signed off the air for the last time. A few seconds later Fire Coordinator Keith

Barber signed on the air using the call signal "Allegany County KKV-461." Also present at that humble beginning were dispatcher Charlie McGill from Whitesville, Dave Jennings from Belfast, Bill Jones from Wellsville, and Craig Braack from Almond. Mr. Barber served as fire coordinator from January of 1979 until December 31, 2001. Mr. Barber died on March 12, 2002. Angelica Fire Chief Paul Gallman was appointed fire coordinator effective January 1, 2002.

"KKV-461 Is on the air!" Keith Barber (standing) congratulating Charlie McGill.

The first use of 9-1-1 in the county was in Wellsville for the local telephone exchange of 593. This started in the very early 1970s and proved its worth during the Flood of 1972. The basic 9-1-1 system, used in the Wellsville 593 exchange only, required the caller to give specific details and location of the incident to the dispatcher. To meet new requirements of New York State, Allegany County implemented the Enhanced 9-1-1 system, commonly known as E-9-1-1 on October 18, 1996. This system has central dispatch from Belmont with an emergency backup system in Wellsville. The first full-time dispatchers were Margo Jennings, Althea Smith, and Randy Swarthout. This improvement now gave the dispatcher the location of the call on a computer screen in addition to the verbal message, thereby enabling faster responses in potentially life-threatening situations. The Wellsville Police and Fire Dispatch Center still maintain their own dispatch system for most of the Town and Village of Wellsville emergency calls.

Communication problems have plagued the Fire Service due to our topography. To rectify this situation, the county installed additional transmission towers in the intervening years. A total of seven towers are in operation today: Joyce Hill in Andover, Corbin Hill in Belmont, Fillmore, Birdsall, Alfred, White Hill in Alma, and in Cuba. The dispatcher now has the benefit of choosing a tower nearest the incident location to better serve those involved. In the 1960ss and 1970s, most fire departments purchased home monitors to notify personnel of emergencies. Over the last few years, these departments have switched to individual pagers.

The old Wellville City Hall burned on April 1, 1954.

It is not practical to mention the many significant fires that have occurred over the years in Allegany County. The superb gifts of the volunteers are simply too numerous to count. Due to their significance in bringing about major change, two fires are worthy of specific mention.

The hamlet of Oramel in the Town of Caneadea was the scene of a major blaze in 1937. A trash fire got out of control due to excessive wind, resulting in the loss of six houses, several other structures, and damage to the Methodist Church. The only major, readily available water supply was the Genesee River, many hundreds of yards away. The efforts of seven neighboring fire companies in securing this water source were quickly hampered by their inability to connect their hoses due to different thread sizes. This disaster prompted the adoption of standard thread size on all firefighting apparatus and fire hose in the county, a change beneficial to all.

The other fire of note was the April 1, 1954 disaster when the building in Wellsville commonly called "Old City Hall" burned. Although Wellsville has never been a city, this name was used for many years. This structure, built in 1894, housed only the Fire Department and its loss caused fire equipment to be housed in local barns and garages until a new facility was erected. On March 3, 1956, the department moved into its new headquarters called the Community Building on Park Avenue. Construction of the four-lane arterial necessitated moving again and the current Fire Department headquarters and Police Station were both built at the same time. The Fire Hall was first occupied on September 15, 1971.

The Short Tract Volunteer Fire Department in the Town of Granger claims a worthy distinction: they were the first department in the county to accept women as full members. A May 4, 1964 *Olean Times-*

Monument Dedication speakers: Senator Pat McGee, George Cotton, Jeff Luckey, County Legislature Chairman Ed Sherman, Assemblyman Dan Burling, Assemblywoman Cathy Young, Bill Heaney, Tommy Thompson, Dave Edwards, and Donn Lang. (Photo courtesy of John Babbitt)

Herald article stated: ". . . after a long debate and the vote was counted, any lady of the community, who was interested was allowed to join the fire company since the town was short on manpower during the day. Eighteen ladies who joined the company were quickly enrolled in the Essentials of Firemanship Class." Deputy Fire Coordinator Don Bledsoe remarked that he "saw the Short Tract venture as hopefully establishing a precedent that other rural volunteer fire companies, similarly short-handed during regular working hours, might well follow."

The Allegany County Volunteer Firemen's Association honored their heritage and future by dedicating a memorial on the front lawn of the Allegany County Court House in Belmont on November 15, 2003. The impetus for this memorial is the September 11, 2001 attacks on the United States. The sacrifices made by firefighters inspired three men to form a committee to spearhead a fundraising campaign: Houghton Chief Dave Edwards, First Assistant Fillmore Chief Tommy Thompson, and First Assistant Short Tract Chief Jeff Luckey. They wanted a memorial dedicated to the firemen of the past, present, and future, and to their respective families.

This committee, working with the Allegany County Volunteer Firemen's Association, George Cotton from the Friendship Volunteer Fire Deprtment, and Donn Lang from the Alfred Station Volunteer Fire Department, started fundraising efforts. This consisted primarily of marketing artist Ann Vaclavik's prints of the memorial design and the selling of border blocks and bricks forming the memorial. The latter would be inscribed according to the donor's wishes.

The Allegany County Board of Legislators demonstrated its support by purchasing the first border block and granting permission to erect the memorial on county property. The dedication ceremony started with the presentation of a large American flag carried by representatives of all twenty-eight county fire departments. A major highlight of the dedication was an address delivered by Fire Coordinator Paul Gallman, tracing the history of the Volunteer Firemen's Association.

According to the committee, the successful completion of the memorial is also the beginning of another campaign. This new goal is the raising of necessary funds to start and maintain the Allegany County Firefighters Scholarship Fund. Its purpose is to assist firefighters or their children who wish to attend college.

Office of Emergency Services

The Office of Emergency Services, originally known as the Office of Civil Defense and Natural Disaster from 1950 until 1980, had its first headquarters in the basement of the Wellsville Post Office on Pearl Street. Charles Covill served as the first director from 1950 until 1952, a part-time position. Hurricane Agnes in 1972 immediately demonstrated the need to enhance emergency response communications and operations. In 1973, the position of director was made full-time. A new emergency operations center opened in the new County Office Building in 1976. Federal matching funds were secured for this location.

Directors since Mr. Covill included Bob Brown from 1952 until 1954, Bob Coulter from 1954 until 1979 and Art Button from 1979 until 1982. John Tucker was then appointed director and he serves in that capacity today. In 1981, Brenda Witter was hired as account/clerk typist. Michael Barney was hired as assistant director in 2004. Since John Tucker's appointment in 1982, Allegany County has been affected nine times by federally declared disasters. A total of approximately $17 million has been received in federal and state disaster assistance.

Allegany County Civil Defense Rescue Squad

This volunteer organization was formed in the early 1950s as a result of public anxiety over the perceived Communist threat. With the "red scare" affecting people's desires for security, a la Senator McCarthy, local measures were implemented under the initial direction of town supervisors. The Allegany County Civil Defense Rescue Squad was founded in 1960 under the leadership of Wellsville Town Supervisor Richard Embser, Robert Coulter, and James and Lewis Cicerello, with the latter serving as first chief. It officially started operations in January of 1961 funded by Allegany County. Mr. Embser operated Embser's

Civil Defense Rescue vehicles parked at their headquarters on Route 417 West, 1986.

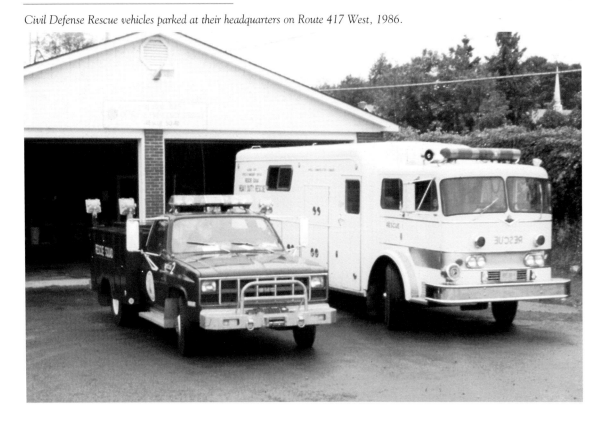

Funeral Home and in those days such businesses also provided ambulance service. Mr. Embser saw the need for a heavy-duty rescue vehicle, separate from the funeral home ambulance service. He then became a leading figure in the squad's formation. Their first headquarters were at the old Sinclair Refinery site on South Brooklyn Avenue in Wellsville. A former Sinclair Refinery Fire Department truck, refurbished by Fred Bell, was put into service as their first vehicle. Lewis Cicerello served as chief until 1975 and his brother Jim served until 1994. On July 13, 1980, Jim Cicerello was presented a medal of honor, the highest award offered by the rescue squad. In the fall of 1980, they moved their headquarters to a site on Route 417 West, just east of the North Highland intersection. They remained there until 1994 when they merged with the Wellsville Volunteer Ambulance Corps. Chris Eldridge became chief of the Rescue Corps division of the ambulance service. This merger was necessitated due to funding cuts by Allegany County. With the construction of the Riverwalk Plaza, their old building was razed.

Emergency Medical Services in Allegany County
A BRIEF HISTORY
BY DR. DAVID P. SCHWERT

Prehospital emergency care for the citizens of Allegany County became fully developed during the last third of the twentieth century. This era saw the development of organized community ambulance services, the training of volunteer personnel in emergency care, the establishment of a communications system between ambulances and hospitals, and an overall system that has evolved to serve the emergency medical needs of the rural population before they are treated in the hospitals.

Prior to 1967 there were a few ambulance services within the county. Alfred, for example, had an ambulance that was operated by the local Fire Department with volunteers receiving their training from Red Cross courses that were offered at various times of the year. In most communities, the ambulance services were offered by the local funeral home whose hearse was converted into an ambulance with the addition of a rooftop red light and perhaps a siren. Those funeral home vehicles were the only choice since they were designed to transport bodies—certainly not elegant, but at the time functional for the needs of the community.

In 1967 the New York State Legislature passed the Emergency Medical Services Act, which phased out the use of hearses as transport vehicles and prescribed the development of community-based ambulance services. This was a massive commitment for the small rural communities because it meant not only acquiring a vehicle but also training personnel, all of whom were volunteers (frequently members of the local fire department). Ambulances of that era were of the "limousine" type, essentially hearse-type vehicles in which the rear compartment was adapted to transport one to four patients. The ambulance purchased in 1969 by the A. E. Crandall Hook and Ladder Company in Alfred was on a Cadillac chassis and could accommodate up to four patients: two in stretchers on the floor and two hanging in folding stretchers from the ceiling. The ambulance squad soon learned that with four patients there was no room for the attendant and no way to care for the patients en route to the hospital. Equipment included oxygen, suction, various bandaging and splinting devices, and several different stretchers. One patient and one attendant allowed for monitoring and treatment in relative comfort. Communications with the hospital involved relaying information through a dispatcher; in the fire department vehicles, this meant going through the fire service communications center in Andover. These ambulances were fast, provided a comfortable ride (especially important for trauma patients), and were a giant first step as Allegany County communities worked toward providing their own prehospital care.

This disaster drill took place at the rest area just north of the old Erie Bridge near Belfast, late 1970s.

The first state-sponsored training for county ambulance personnel began in March of 1967 with the development of a thirty-two-hour Medical Emergency Technician course that was held at Alfred State College. Over 120 volunteers from around the county were enrolled in that course (it seemed so long at the time!) and learned the rudiments of evaluating an ill or injured patient, interpreting vital signs, treating various medical conditions, and, very importantly, safely transporting the patients. Often the most difficult chore was that of moving the patients from where they were found—upstairs bedroom, wrecked car, bottom of a steep ravine—to where the ambulance was parked. Class members were used to practice on so that fledgling METs (as they were call at that time) would learn not only how to handle the patients in various difficult situations but also how it felt to be transported down a steep set of stairs (never head-first), removed from the back-seat floor of a car, and carried up a steep bank (often at night when it was raining or snowing). New METs also learned water rescue in the college's swimming pool, emergency childbirth techniques, and the restraint of patients who were belligerent or uncooperative. At the end of the first course, over 120 newly certified METs went back to their communities and their limousine-type vehicles to begin what would develop into sixteen ambulance services within the county. Their certification was good for two years at which time a refresher course of approximately half the duration of the original course was required. These early courses and the hard work of these students provided the foundation of the Emergency Medical Services system that serves Allegany County to this day.

The early 1970s brought many improvements: First the limousine-type ambulances (really nothing more than modified hearses) were replaced by vehicles designed from the ground up to fit the needs of prehospital emergency care. These included the Type I ambulance which was essentially a box-type compartment fitted onto the back of a truck-type chassis. This design allowed for a tremendous increase in storage space for the ever-increasing items of equipment and for increased work area for personnel to care for patient en route to the hospital. Wonderful for their space, these Type I vehicles were horrible in the quality of ride since they were built on stiffly sprung truck chasses. Type III ambulances were large vans outfitted for patient care. While not quite as roomy as the Type I, they were a good compromise between working space and ride. Most communities, to this day, use Type I and Type III vehicles.

Also in the early 1970s the METs of the earlier era became EMTs, Emergency Medical Technicians—a change in designation that reflected the increasing complexity of prehospital care and the extended length of required training. The EMT course first doubled and then tripled in length, allowing for more extensive training and coordination but creating a greater burden for class members since these volunteers were now required to attend many more classes over a greater period of time. Exams for certification of EMTs became standardized throughout New York State, following standards established by the federal government. Volunteers worked long and hard to earn EMT certification then returned to their communities to devote long and difficult hours helping their fellow citizens in their time of need. A great deal of time and sacrifice went into this project reflecting not only the large number of patients that were well served but also by the continuing need for training and recertification to maintain the EMT designation.

One of the more interesting phases of EMT training in the 1970s and 1980s was simulating mass-casualty disaster situations. While a seriously ill or injured patient (they were never called victims) provided a challenge for the local rescue service, a multiple-patient situation such as an automobile accident, school bus crash, or some such scenario needed to be carefully planned. An organization in Buffalo called the First Aid Simulation Team (FAST) was composed of volunteer members trained to act as casualties, complete with realistic wounds, fractures, shock, and vocal effects. Each EMT course concluded with training for a mass casualty disaster. Up to thirty FAST Team members would serve as patients in a simulated large-scale disaster, and the whole EMT class would respond. Events that were staged included school bus accidents, an airplane crash, and a multiple-casualty "fall" off of the railroad trestle bridge in Belfast. Since the early moments of any disaster are confusing at best, the concept of "triage" was practiced to sort the patients and provide the greatest good for the greatest number of patients. Ambulances and equipment were staged near the triage area and the injured were evaluated and treated there; the most critical were the first to be transported to area hospitals where the emergency departments activated their disaster plans and fully participated in this exercise. These were exciting events with police and fire departments actively participating. What first looked like "organized chaos" became a well-orchestrated rehearsal for an event that everyone hoped would never occur.

From the early beginnings forty years ago, prehospital emergency care has expanded to include sophisticated techniques of auto extrication, cardiac defibrillation, on-scene IV and drug administration, and medical helicopter evacuation—all of which have greatly increased the hours and quality of training. The men and women who serve with the Allegany County volunteer ambulance services are to be admired and thanked for their countless hours of training, the quality of care provided, and the cheerful, compassionate spirit in which they treat and comfort those in need of emergency care.

The Critical Incident Stress Crisis Support Team

Despite excellent firefighting and EMT instruction available locally, incidents sometimes occur that volunteers simply aren't trained or equipped to handle emotionally. On occasion, fires or life and death situations on ambulance calls create tremendous stress for the responding volunteers.

In December of 1986, three people were killed in a devastating motor vehicle accident in Alfred. In response to the unexpected emotional counseling needs for several emergency personnel who were involved in this incident, the need for a peer-led emotional support group was realized. Under a joint effort by the Office of Emergency Services and the Health Department, the Allegany County Crisis Support team was organized in early 1987. Initial members were Bonnelyn Buckley and Chris Johnson from the Health Department, Barbara Fletcher of Alfred State College, Sue Wolfer from Fillmore, and Craig Braack of the Almond Ambulance Squad. All were certified EMTs.

If the fire chief or ambulance captain in charge of a tragic incident felt the crisis team was needed for a "debriefing session" upon completion of the incident, the team was activated through County Fire Control. In the intervening years, other qualified volunteers joined the team and have responded to several dozen debriefing sessions in Allegany County and a few in four neighboring counties.

chapter 13

"UNLUCKY 13," DOOM AND GLOOM, DISASTERS–NATURAL AND OTHERWISE

Despite the best of prevention efforts, misfortune and disaster will occasionally befall us. When these accidents and disasters occur, whatever their cause or extent, the indomitable spirit of mankind will surface to rebuild our temporarily shaken world. Sometimes our travails are small, sometimes they are massive, but they all have one thing in common—in the end, we realize we simply are at the mercy of nature or "acts of God."

The residents of Allegany County certainly have experienced "their share" of disaster and misfortune. Sadly, only a few major or historically significant events can be covered.

Ordeals by Water

EARLY FLOODS: Floods have plagued mankind since the dawn of civilization. Allegany County certainly has been no exception. The first flood of significance in the twentieth century occurred in early July of 1902 exceeding all previous records. Damage was extensive throughout the county with many bridges and railroad beds washed away.

Water was six feet deep on Fillmore streets. In the hamlet of Mills, all businesses were washed away, leaving it a farming community only. Twelve houses were washed away in Angelica, with Main Street mostly a scene of wrack and ruin. Three iron bridges were taken out as well. Along the line of the Erie Railroad, damage was extensive in the Andover area with a landslide at Alfred. An Erie bridge suffered major damage in Scio. In Belmont, a pond washed out taking with it sixty thousand feet of logs and the railroad trestle at Clark Brothers. Damage was also extensive throughout the village of Wellsville and the hamlet of Whitesville.

Flash floods hit the central part of the county and Angelica was particularly hard hit in 1913 and again in 1916. The most devastating flood of the first half of the nineteenth century occurred in early July of 1935, paralleling the disastrous flood of 1902. A major difference was that this flood struck during the worst part of the Great Depression. With high unemployment and localized pockets of poverty, this flood had devastating effects and left a lasting impression on the residents of the Southern Tier. Every genera-

◄ *High water on Olean Street in Angelica, March 1913*

Top: This view from behind the Allegany County Courthouse shows the Belmont Fire Hall in the Flood of 1972.

Middle: The Genesee River flows over the bridge by the Belmont Fire Hall during the Flood of 1972. (Photo courtesy of Bill Greene Jr.)

Bottom: In the Town of Hume the Flood of 1972 damaged the Lattice Bridge, the oldest bridge in Allegany County. The bridge is now closed.

tion suffers an experience around which they mark time ever after. The Flood of 1935 was the defining natural disaster of that generation.

In the village of Almond, a man of twenty-five years was supporting his disabled mother and infirm sister. He bartered with the owner of a barn to tear it down, making two piles of lumber, with the owner taking his choice. The remaining lumber was the man's pay. The owner was to make his choice on Monday, July 8, and the flood struck on July 7. Both men lost everything.

With World War II barely underway, the region again suffered a major flood in mid-July of 1942. Six bridges were taken out on county roads. The Genesee River reached a record crest of eleven feet, five inches at the Wellsville Water and Light Plant. The Erie Railroad had to divert all trains over its Buffalo Division lines due to many washouts throughout the county.

FLOOD OF 1972: For the latter half of the twentieth century, the defining moment for adults came in June of 1972. Just the mention of the words *Hurricane Agnes* elicits serious responses from all who were here during that fateful week. The Flood of 1972 replaced the Flood of 1942 as the point of reference in people's lives.

Weather forecasts of the previous few days called for rain as the hurricane's remnants would pass over the Northeast United States. However, this was not the case as the massive front stalled and over thirteen inches of rain fell during a three-day period. The majority fell during the night of Tuesday, June 21. This proved to be the most destructive and expensive storm in the Northeast's history. In those five days 28.1 trillion gallons of water fell on New

Debris from the Flood of 1972 blocks the entrance to the East Hughes Street Bridge in Belfast.

Above: The Windus Bridge over the Genesee River in the Town of Amity was badly affected by the Flood or 1972.

Right: These buildings on the Potter farm were barely above water during the Flood of 1972.

York and Pennsylvania. Property damage reached $2.5 billion, about 200,000 people were left homeless and 118 people died. Federal aid of $694 million was given to New York State and $1.2 billion was given to Pennsylvania.

There were two areas of major concern during this period. Most immediately in danger was the Village of Almond, which was evacuated late Wednesday morning with residents being sent to Alfred Almond Central School. This was necessitated by the collapse of two sluices carrying the Karr Valley Creek under the newly constructed massive earthen embankment just west of the village, turning it into a "shaky dam." The embankment was part of the construction of the Southern Tier Expressway, Route 17. The collapse of the sluices created a lake sixty feet deep, a quarter mile wide, and one mile long. New York State Department of Transportation engineers feared the embankment would give way, destroying the village. On duty state trooper T. D. Root said: "It was like looking down the barrel of a loaded shotgun. If that road had collapsed, it would've been a big ol' tidal wave. There wouldn't have been anything left of Almond." After six days living in the school, residents were allowed to return to their homes.

The second area of concern was the Village of Wellsville. By daylight Wednesday, June 22, flooding in the village was severe and getting worse. All schools, businesses, and non-emergency facilities were closed. Many residences and the Wellsville Nursing Home were evacuated with churches being used as shelters. The Genesee River crested at twenty-three feet, sixteen feet above normal. Early Friday morning, even worse flooding occurred and the Genesee crested at twenty-four feet. At 6:50 a.m., five floors of the Jones Memorial Hospital west wing collapsed into the river. All patients and equipment had been safely evacuated. A large section of the nearby Lutheran Church Parish Hall also collapsed. Eye-witness Mrs. Christine Boller of Wellsville described the hospital as "Slowly sliding so effortlessly into the river." Saturday night, the last major infrastructure damage occurred as the West Pearl Street Bridge finally collapsed.

Top: The west wing of the Jones Memorial Hospital in Wellsville collapsed into the river during the flood of 1972.

Bottom: Cars at Lester Chevrolet on South Main Street in Wellsville were under water during the Flood of 1972.

The Flood of 1972 tragically cost three lives, two in Almond and one in Scio with millions of dollars in damage throughout the county. The *Wellsville Daily Reporter* published ten thousand copies of a special twenty-four-page flood history and it sold out within a week. Included were over seven hundred photos and it sold for thirty-five cents.

This view, taken before the Flood of 1972 from West State Street Bridge in Wellsville, is looking north downriver. It shows the beginning of the Genesee River relocation for construction of the "four-lane." The Pearl Street Bridge seen in the distance fell in the Flood of 1972.

Perhaps Gilbert Stinger said it best in his editorial column in the *Olean Times-Herald* on the flood's tenth anniversary entitled: "What Is A Flood?" Stinger so eloquently wrote:

> *It is a rearrangement of things. Things from the cellar to the first floor, to the second floor if you've got a second floor. But mainly a rearrangement of values. Things which were important yesterday, seem less important now, or even not important at all. Is anything more important than for the rain to stop, the water to go down? It is a new mood in town. A coming togetherness because of a giant, tragic drenching that came out of the sky one night and kept coming and coming and filled the creeks and the rivers until the banks could no longer hold it back, and over it came and with it went your favorite chair and your freezer and your TV set and your home and your way of life. These were some of the things I saw or felt during the flood. A flood of sights and sounds and thoughts and feelings which rose with the water, stayed long enough to make words, and now are gone again.*

The Great Cyclone of 1920

One of the worst storms ever to hit the county struck without warning shortly after 10:00 p.m., July 23, 1920. Various accounts called the storm a tornado, a hurricane, or a cyclone. Call it what you want, central parts of the county were devastated. For those affected, this storm was the defining moment of a generation.

It touched down just east of Cuba causing minor damage, continuing in an easterly path through the towns of Friendship and Amity, again causing sporadic damage with several homes destroyed. In the Belmont area, the property of Lew Bentley on Plum Bottom Road was hit hard with his home and barn

destroyed. Here the storm took its first life when the Bentley's infant was pulled from its mother's arms by the wind and killed. Then the storm veered slightly south wreaking havoc through much of the Town of Ward, particularly in Elm Valley on present-day County Road 12. Many additional farmhouses and barns were destroyed. Farmer Carl Will was also killed when a beam from his collapsing house fell on him. Most of the area grain crops were flattened by the storm and orchards uprooted. For the most part, the orchards were not replanted, ending an era of successful commercial apple growing, particularly in the Beech Hill area of the Town of Willing.

The Tornado of 1920 caused great destruction at the McAndrew farm in Elm Valley near Andover.

Buildings were gradually repaired or replaced and people returned to normal as much as possible. As few had insurance to cover this extensive damage, recovery was accomplished at the local level. The Wellsville Red Cross appealed for help and goods. As was the case in times of disaster, relatives, friends, and neighbors pitched in to help. Federal and state relief programs as we know them today were still decades away.

Other Great Winds

Although Allegany County has been plagued by many high winds since, perhaps the experience of the Calcagno family in 2002 best personifies the emotional trauma resulting from losing one's home. On April 28, 2002, retired Allegany County Deputy Sheriff Frank Calcagno and his wife Janet were returning home in the late afternoon only to be met at a roadblock by deputies and Belfast firefighters. They were told: "Frank, don't be surprised if you don't have a house anymore." This confirmed F-2 tornado left their home in a pile of rubble, and their eighty-by-fifty-foot barn behind the house disappeared without a trace. Ironic is the fact that their dog, chained to a tree next to the house, survived. Nearby mobile homes of Thomas McKelvey and Thomas Fountain and his fiancé Elynn Manhart and two children were also destroyed.

The storm's path took it over Tibbetts Hill Road damaging several structures before destroying the three homes. Hundreds of towering pines up and down the valley were mowed flat by the high winds. There was damage to barns, silos, and trees from Tibbetts Hill to Angelica and West Almond with many utility lines down. Damage and power outages were reported from Rushford, New Hudson, Cuba, Belfast, Angelica, and West Almond.

Tornado-force winds struck on County Road 10, the Vandermark Road in the Town of Ward on Thursday, August 22, 2002. The July 1920 storm had destroyed a house and barn on the site currently

The Canaseraga Fire of 1895 destroyed twenty-four stores, two hotels, the bank, the post office, and thirty-four homes.

lived in by Fred and Joan Sinclair. This latter storm blew onto their home a windbreak of seventy-year-old, eighteen-inch-wide trees. Many acres of adjoining State Forest Land trees were also destroyed. Mr. Sinclair quipped: "I guess we live in Allegany County's own tornado alley."

The Sinclair Fires of 1938 and 1958

While many major fires have scarred Allegany County's landscape, none has been more talked about than the Sinclair Oil Refinery Fire of 1938. Beyond a doubt, this was the largest and most costly fire in the county's history. Simply stated, for the many people who witnessed this conflagration, it became known as "The Fire!" It broke out at 4:00 p.m. Sunday, July 17, and was declared out at 6:30 p.m., Tuesday, July 19. Lives of three spectators were lost when a twenty-five-hundred-barrel tank, containing lube oil and naptha exploded and was hurtled five hundred feet across the Genesee River landing in the midst of a crowd of onlookers. Over one hundred others received minor injuries. The Sinclair Company estimated the loss at $1 million. Almost every fire department in a twenty-five-mile radius was involved with fighting the fire, either directly at the scene or providing stand-by assistance in various fire stations. American LaFrance and Foamite Corporations in Elmira sent a quarter million pounds of Foamite that ultimately succeeded in conquering the fire. Radio bulletins spanned thousands of miles and were soon followed by bold headlines in newspapers from coast to coast. The eyes of the world "literally" watched Wellsville.

The subsequent investigation was not able to pinpoint a cause; speculation abounded however. While it is known the fire started in the centrifuge plant, part of their dewaxing plant, possibly the trouble originated in a pump or in an electric motor. When the "flash" did occur, flames spread instantly devouring the dewaxing plant. Other smaller tanks quickly exploded creating the massive fire. The investigation further concluded that the fire cut electric power lines shutting down the refinery turbines and causing the collapse of the stanchions supporting the steam lines. Without power, pumps were down and the water lines without pressure. Without power, without steam and without water, the entire refinery was at the mercy of the rampant flames.

The Sinclair Corporation rebuilt the affected areas. However, fire again struck on February 9 and 10, 1958. These losses combined with the decline of crude oil production from local wells brought about the decision to close the facility.

The Alfred Ag Tech Barn Fires

In 1907, New York State officially created an agricultural college at Alfred commonly called Alfred State College today. For many years it was also Alfred State Agricultural and Technical Institute, still called or known by many as simply, "Ag Tech." Being an agricultural facility, building a working dairy barn was a necessity. In the fall of 1910, a large barn was built on the present location of the college's bus barn on North Main Street. Almost finished, with the builder's tools still inside, the barn burned on December 31, 1910. They built a duplicate barn on the original foundation, completing it in 1911. This barn served the needs of the college until it burned on October 2, 1960. The barn was destroyed, but all cattle and records were saved. The records consisted of valuable dairy breed registry data, some of these irreplaceable. They were saved when the safe in which they were stored was pulled from the smoking ruins by a tractor. The decision to rebuild was quickly made but in a different location.

The significance of this fire is that the college created a greatly expanded farm and barn complex of relatively fireproof material. The site they chose is on Route 244, a few hundred yards west of the old site. This further enabled the college to greatly increase the size of its facility as the open space allowed new curricula in agriculture technology.

The Ice Storm of 1991

Sunday night, March 3, 1991, proved to be the beginning of a major electrical outage for most of Allegany County. A very unusual weather phenomenon called a "temperature inversion" occurred, caus-

Top: A couple dressed in white, complete with hats, watches from the grassy hillside as the smoke billows from the Sinclair Refinery Fire of 1938.

Bottom: Aftermath of the Sinclair Refinery Fire of 1938.

ing a major ice storm throughout the Genesee River Valley. Snow fell on far Western New York while Central New York received rain. In our area, with cold temperatures at ground level and warm temperatures at higher levels, rain started falling, turning to ice upon contact with exposed surfaces.

As heavy, ice-laden branches snapped liked kindling wood, falling on power lines, electrical service was disrupted throughout the county in the early morning hours of March 4. At dawn, the devastation became apparent and word quickly spread that the loss of service would be, in the words of the power companies serving the county, "an extended outage." This turned out to be quite the understatement. For those able to stay in their homes, cooking on wood stoves and dining by candlelight became the norm. Battery supplies ran low.

Top: *Ice Storm of 1936 showing the Almond High School, now Mullen Carpets.*

Bottom: *Ice Storm of March 13, 1991, with downed power lines and pole on Main Street in Almond.*

First to respond to various needs in our communities were our volunteer fire and ambulance personnel checking on home-bound residents and those with medical needs requiring electricity. Fire halls quickly filled as the residents sought the basic amenities of home that were available due to operating generators. Allegany County authorities quickly enacted a "state of emergency" banning all unnecessary travel. This stayed in effect until March 14. The three power companies serving the county brought in work crews from the surrounding states to augment their crews. On Friday, March 8, while addressing the County Legislature's Public Works Committee, County Department of Public Works Superintendent Richard Young stated, "Canaseraga, Almond, Alfred, and Andover areas were hit the worst." He further stated his department had spent about $22,000 so far in employee time and equipment in dealing with the effects of the storm. Lastly he added: "We'll be cleaning up storm damage for a long time to come."

President Bush declared Western New York a federal disaster area which made the affected area eligible for three programs to help individuals, business people, and farmers. Most affected areas in the county had power restored within a few days. However, it was over a week for some remote areas to regain

Wellsville's Fassett House, circa 1915, looking south. Automobiles outnumber the horse-drawn carriages on the street, and everybody has on a hat. Note the elegant people on the second-floor porch.

power. Perhaps best stating the extent of damage in our area was a "thank you" letter sent to all agencies involved in recovering from the effects of the storm. The letter, written by Fred Marks, Hornell Division manager of New York State Electric and Gas, stated: "In the NYSEG affected areas, there were twenty-seven transmission lines, twenty-four substations, and fifty-two distribution circuits put out of action. It took years to develop that electrical system, and then we had to put it back together in a week. Thanks to a magnificent community effort, the job went smoothly and quickly."

The Fassett House

The Fassett House in Wellsville was built by Isaac W. Fassett in 1872 on North Main Street. It quickly became a fixture in the community, serving primarily as a hotel and dining facility. Many public, political, and social events encompassing a wide area were held in the hotel's dining area and its popular "Gold Room." Changes in America's traveling patterns caused a drop in hotel clientele with the facility falling into a gradual state of disrepair. In the 1990s, after changing hands many times, the upper floors were made into apartments by its last owner, Henry Bauer. The "Gold Room" became a laundromat and the first floor housed several businesses.

On the below freezing night of January 19, 2003, about twenty residents had to be evacuated from their apartments due to flooding from burst water pipes. It was estimated that between 128,000 and 150,000 gallons of water caused extensive damage throughout the wood-frame structure. The structure's death knell was sounded the night of April 29, 2003, when firefighters from Wellsville and several mutual aid responding departments found flames on all three floors. There were no water, power, or residents in the building when the flames broke out.

Deemed structurally unsound by officials, the building was ultimately condemned. Demolition started in February 2005. In addition to the loss of a residential building and the displacement of businesses, the historic Fassett's demise leaves a gaping hole on Wellsville's Main Street.

chapter 14

THE GREAT OUTDOORS

Just saying "The Great Outdoors" evokes many thoughts of enjoyable sporting and environmental pursuits readily available in Allegany County for most all age and ability levels. The county is blessed with sparkling waters for fishing or a quiet canoe venture on the scenic Genesee River. Verdant forests abound with flora and fauna. The colors of autumn are second to none. The lush, green hiking trails are also beautiful when the snows of winter welcome the cross-country skier.

Many of the county's beautiful nature-related areas today became public lands due to the effects of the Great Depression on local farmers. Dozens of farms failed with New York State subsequently purchasing the land. These 46,329 acres of State Forest in the northern half of the county have an intriguing history.

Civilian Conservation Corps—"Mr. Roosevelt's Tree Army"

I propose to create a Civilian Conservation Corps to be used in simple work. More important, however, than the material gain will be the moral and spiritual value of such work.

—Franklin D. Roosevelt, March 9, 1933

This quotation was part of President Roosevelt's speech to an emergency session of Congress wherein he proposed to recruit thousands of unemployed young men, enroll them in a peacetime army, and send them into battle against destruction and erosion of our natural resources, primarily caused by droughts in the early 1930s. By the end of 1935, there were almost twenty-seven hundred camps across the country with enrollees numbering just over 506,000. They were paid $30 a month with a mandatory $25 allotment check sent to the families back home. In camp, the enrollees were under the supervision of the Army. The Department of Forests and Waters was in charge of scheduling crews to work in the fields and woods and along the streams. An Army captain or first lieutenant was in charge of each camp and was assisted by two lieutenants and a top sergeant in charge of the mess hall. Officers were addressed as "sir" but not saluted. Men wore a uniform designed for the Corps and lived in army-style barracks. The eating arrangements were copied after the Army and every morning the whole camp stood formation. Permission from the camp commander was needed to leave camp.

◀ *Parade Float in Andover for July 4, 1909, of the Modern Woodmen of America. The MWA was one of our earliest environmental organizations.*

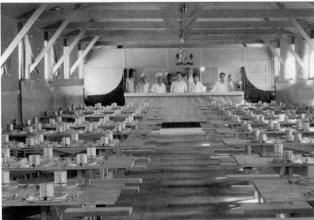

Top: Centerville Civilian Conservation Corps (CCC) Camp

Middle: Interior of West Almond CCC Camp Mess Hall, circa 1934

Bottom: West Almond CCC Camp on Dedication Day, September 26, 1934

Allegany County was home to two CCC camps: Lost Nation Camp in Centerville, camp S-126, Company 1291; and Camp S-92, named St. Helena in West Almond that was home to Engineering Company 268. Buildings included barracks, mess hall, and shops for carpentry, tools, machinery, maintenance, repairs, etc. Enrollees planted thousands of acres of trees consisting of oaks, pines, black cherry, American elm, larch, Norway maple, black walnut, and red ash. The Jersey Hill fire tower was constructed in the winter of 1934–35 and torn down in 1987 due to maintenance costs and liability hazards. The other major construction project was the building of Palmers Pond in the winter of 1935–36. This was for recreation purposes and as a water supply for forest fires. There were three camps in Letchworth State Park and the men built much of the park's infrastructure. Across New York State they planted 221 million trees, cleared 391 miles of truck trails, and constructed seventy-three vehicle bridges.

Race would prove to be a problem with segregation still rampant in the country. At first some camps were integrated, but in 1935 all became segregated. This was the case in West Almond in 1941, when white enrollees were detailed to camps in Attica and Peekskill. A small article in the November 11, 1941 issue of the *Wellsville Daily Reporter* stated: "A 150 Negro detachment from the abandoned Beaver Dams camp at Monterey took over the CCC camp in West Almond." The article further explained this change was made due to decreased enrollments. The end came on March 30, 1942, when the camp was disbanded. At this time, Congress stopped funding the CCC due to World War II.

Today, one building remains on the West Almond site and is known as the West Almond Field Operations Maintenance Center, New York State Department of Environmental Conservation (NYS-DEC). Employment here ranges from about five in winter to about nine in summer. From the

This West Almond Fire Tower was erected by the CCC in the winter of 1933–1934 and torn down in the early 1980s.

Centerville Camp, one building remains, but not on its original site. Most recently it has been known as "Sam's Dance Hall." The lasting legacy of the CCC can be seen today in thousands of acres of New York State forestlands used for a multitude of recreational purposes. The economic benefits of the CCC efforts in reforestation have resulted in surface erosion control and income from harvesting trees.

NYS-DEC Wildlife Management Areas

There are four such areas in the county owned by the DEC. These areas are:

HANGING BOG: The DEC brochure states: "The Hanging Bog Wildlife Management Area (WMA) located in the town of New Hudson is named for the large natural bog on the property. The tract encompasses 4,571 acres of rolling hills, extensive forestlands and marshes. Since 1948, management practices have included conifer plantation establishment, thinning of plantations, selective and clear-cutting of hardwoods, leasing of croplands, planting wildlife shrubs and developing small marshes, ponds and potholes. All these practices provide nesting, feeding, and cover habitat for wildlife. The many wild species found here provide ample recreational opportunities for hunters, photographers and nature observers."

GENESEE VALLEY: The Wildlife Management Area in the Town of Granger is the newest in the county having been created in 2004. The site consists of 580 acres of river bottomlands, abandoned farmland, and upland hardwoods. About one-third of the site is in Livingston County and two-thirds is in Allegany County. The land was a gift to the State from Gary Russell.

KEANEY SWAMP: The DEC brochure for this area essentially says the same as for Hanging Bog except it is located in the Town of Birdsall and contains 707 acres, mostly natural wetlands. The primary management objective of this area is to maintain a quality wetland habitat for waterfowl through control of beaver population, ditching, and mowing. Credit must be given to the DEC personnel Mike Ermer, Russ Biss, and Matt Perkins who arranged for and directed the extensive, quality improvements in Keaney Swamp from 2003 to 2005.

Top: Keaney Swamp Department of Environmental Conservation (DEC) restoration project on May 19, 2004

Bottom: Dedication of Andover Ponds restoration project, October 22, 1994: Left to right are unidentified, County Legislature Chair John Walchli, State Senator Pat McGee, Andover Town Supervisor Karl Graves, Chuck Booker, U.S. Soil and Water Representative Bob Pederson, Judy Scott, unidentified U.S. Fish and Wildlife representative, and County Legislator Keith Palmiter.

RATTLESNAKE HILL: Most of this area lies in Livingston County while about a third is in the Town of Grove in northeast Allegany County. It consists of fifty-one hundred acres of upland tract of mature woodland, overgrown fields, conifer plantations, and open meadows. Appropriately the area is named after the Timber Rattlesnake that may occasionally be found in the more remote sections.

While not open to the public on a regular basis, the Rushford DEC Camp is one of two such environment-oriented camps in the state. Started in the early 1950s as a camp for boys, it became coed in the 1980s. The Rushford Camp is operated by Albany DEC personnel from late June to late August. About sixty campers attend per week.

Viewing Nature at Its Best

ANDOVER PONDS: Originally a single body of water created by a dam, the Andover Pond was divided into four separate bodies in the early 1850s when the Erie Railroad was constructed. Cottages

Moss Lake in the fall

dotted the banks for summer leisure. In the winter, bands played while skaters frolicked on the ice.

The dam was ignored for many years and concern for its stability grew, particularly after the damaging effects of the Flood of 1972. Maintenance responsibility was a "muddy issue" in oft-heated debates between various levels of government and concerned citizens.

Finally, having enough of "government bureaucracy," Andover residents Judy Scott and Chuck Booker took it upon themselves to raise money to replace the dam, ultimately saving the ponds. Through fifteen different, major fundraisers, $100,000 was raised. Major work was performed by the Allegany County Department of Public Works. In August 1998, a ribbon-cutting ceremony was held for the restored Andover Wetlands Project with federal, state, county, and local officials presiding.

BROWN'S MARSH: Approximately two miles east of Wellsville on Route 417 is an environmentally sensitive area named after the late Ruth (Farnum) Brown, formerly of Wellsville. She gave this area to the Western New York Land Conservancy in the late 1990s. In March of 2001, the Land Conservancy announced the acquisition of two adjoining parcels. Otis Eastern Corporation, a pipeline construction company, donated thirty-seven acres within the Dyke Creek flood plain/wetland area to the Conservancy. This property is next to Brown's Marsh Preserve and connects to an eighty-four-acre parcel called the Mulholland Tract, which was owned by Charles P. Joyce Jr., president of Otis Eastern. Mr. Joyce sold this tract to the Conservancy. These acquisitions created a total of 306 acres preserved through the stewardship of the Western New York Land Conservancy.

GREENWAY TRAIL: The Genesee Valley Greenway follows the towpath of the former Genesee Valley Canal (1840–1878) and railbed of the Pennsylvania Railroad, Rochester Branch (1882–1963), passing through five counties, several villages, and seventeen townships. Surviving remnants of these fascinating forms of transportation offer tantalizing glimpses of life in the 1800s in the Genesee Valley as the trail winds through shaded woodlands, farmlands, and peaceful valleys. The proposed ninety-mile trail from Rochester to Cuba, and possibly to Hinsdale in Cattaraugus County, is not yet complete. As of this writing, about fifty-five miles are completed, primarily in the northern sections, with about seven miles open in Allegany County.

MOSS LAKE: Located off Sand Hill Road in the Town of Caneadea, this is a unique ecosystem in the county. A myriad of plants native to both northern and southern climates, including four carnivorous species, exist side by side in the glacier-carved hollow known as Moss Lake Nature Sanctuary. Found here is a rich deposit of peat that was mined extensively, creating the present-day lake. Mining operations ceased in 1956 and the land was for sale. The threat of commercial development was looming and Dr. Crystal Rork, a biology professor from Houghton College, spearheaded a drive to form the Western New York Chapter of the Nature Conservancy. This international organization buys ecologically sensitive and threatened areas; thus preserving them for restricted public use. The new chapter was formed in 1957 and purchased the land from Mr. and Mrs. Orville Hotchkiss in 1958. The formal dedication took place on June 21, 1958, with 150 members and friends present.

Alfred University football team captain, November 19, 1906

Moss Lake is open daylight hours only for public use. The Western New York Chapter of the Conservancy built a boardwalk on the bog enabling visitors to better view and photograph rare plants. However, to maintain nature's integrity, picking or removing any plant is strictly forbidden.

The Sporting Life

TEAM SPORTS: Until recent times, team sports as are commonly known, weren't available until junior high or senior high. However the concept of winning at higher levels has created the need of teaching elementary children the basics of team and individual sports at a much younger age. Today, there are many school and non-school-sponsored leagues for most sports at all age levels and certainly for both girls and boys. The programs start with "pee wee" type leagues and are available all the way through senior high school.

COLLEGE LEVEL SPORTS: In the last fifty years or so, the Athletic Departments at Alfred State College, Alfred University, and Houghton College have expanded tremendously, offering their students a wide range of sports opportunities. All three institutions have built state-of-the-art fields, pools, and gymnasiums with the necessary equipment.

ADULTS: Participation in team sports no longer needs to end for adults because throughout Allegany County numerous sports leagues and opportunities exist.

"WHITE TAIL COUNTRY": The sport of hunting can easily be considered a major business in the county. We are consistently one of the leading counties in New York State for the number of deer taken each year. According to NYS-DEC statistics, the Town of Wellsville had the highest buck count in the state—4.9 bucks per square mile. Many hundreds of cabins owned by nonresidents dot the countryside. However, the number of licensed hunters in New York State has dropped over the past few years, as has the number of deer taken, according to DEC statistics.

White tail deer hunting in New York State was not allowed from the very early 1900s until 1939, as deer had been extirpated from the region. When the deer population had reached a manageable number, hunting season was then resumed. One can imagine hunters' excitement at the beginning of the 1939 big game season as bucks with mammoth racks were abundant. Two New York State records were established that season for big bucks. Roosevelt Luckey took a buck in the Town of Hume that measured 198 and three-eighths points on the Boone and Crockett Club scale. This record stands today. The other record buck was taken by Homer Boylan in the Town of Burns, and this buck was scored on the Northeast Big Buck scale. A buck taken in 2004 by Andrew Carney of Canaseraga, on the same hill where Boylan bagged his deer, scored higher on the Northeast Big Buck scale.

Small game is also abundant in our area. The varieties of habitat over a large portion of the county offer an ample supply of turkey, pheasant, rabbit, and squirrel. There are also seasons for bow and arrow and black-powder hunting.

Tullar Field in Wellsville, Flood of 1913 (from postcard)

Ski tow at Swain, late 1940s

"TAKE ME OUT TO THE BALLGAME": The Pennsylvania, Ontario, and New York (PONY) League was a Class D League of minor-league professional baseball with local teams in Wellsville and Hornell for much of the 1940s, 1950s, and early 1960s. The Wellsville team was affiliated with the following major league teams: New York Yankees from 1942 to 1946, Boston Red Sox in 1947 and 1948, Nitros in 1949 (independent), Senators in 1950, Rockets in 1951 and 1952 (independent), Milwaukee Braves from 1953 to 1961. Wellsville was out of the league for one year, and affiliated with the Boston Red Sox from 1963 to 1965. All games were played at Tullar Field. In 1967, the field was turned over to the village when Mayor Robert Gardner accepted the deed offered by Bayard C. Tullar, president of the Tullar Field Association. The massive grandstand was soon torn down, making way for the new fire and police headquarters.

During the time of minor-league ball in Wellsville, quite a few players made it to the big-leagues. Among them were Jerry Coleman, Tony Conigliaro, Joe Foy, Charlie Maxwell, Jerry Moses, George Scott, and Charlie Silvera.

The team name *Nitros* would once again surface in the county as organized baseball returned when Wellsville became a franchise member of the Northeast Collegiate Baseball League sanctioned by the National Collegiate Athletic Association and major league baseball. The Wellsville Nitros started play in early June of 1998 with Dick Cuykendall as general manager.

The Nitros changed their name in 2002 to the Allegany County Nitros and moved to Scio in 2003 in order to play night games as well. In 2005, three games will be played at Bolivar. Current president and general manager is Dan Russo.

"It's All Downhill From Here!"

SWAIN SKI AND SNOWBOARD CENTER: This skiing mecca is located in the Town of Grove and claims to be the oldest continuously operated ski area in New York State. It was started in 1947 by Dave and Bina Robinson and is corporately owned today. In the mid-1990s, they installed the first quad lift in the state and the third in the world. Using all their lifts, they can transport eighty-four hundred people up the hill in an hour. When the Robinsons started their business, they depended entirely on natural snow. Today, after spending over $2 million on snowmaking equipment, they completely discount natural snow. According to manager John Gorton, "weather reports of snow only mean I have to plow the parking lots." Several years ago, they added snowboarding and tubing , thereby appealing to the latest sports interests of youth.

Appreciating Nature by Satellite

GEO-CACHING: This activity was born in May of 2000, when the Clinton administration released for civilian use, signals from satellites previously only available to the military. The best way to describe this new use of our environment is that it is a cross between an electronic version of a scavenger hunt and a road rally. By using signals from satellites on handheld GPS (Global Positioning System) units, a geo-cacher finds a logbook in some type of container, often with trinkets. The container had been previously hidden by another geo-cacher. Searchers are encouraged to write in the logbook and later post their results on a website.

Geo-cachers are particularly sensitive to leaving a cache site cleaner than they found it. They are committed to the practice of "CITO," Cache In–Trash Out! These activities allow them to meet, clean up a site, and place a cache as a memorial of the event.

chapter 15

HISTORICAL RESOURCES AND PLACES OF INTEREST

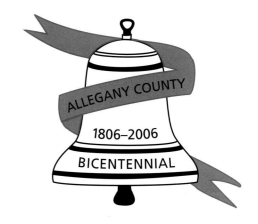

ALLEGANY COUNTY
1806–2006
BICENTENNIAL

National and State Registers

Authorized under the National Preservation Act of 1966, the National Register is part of a national program to coordinate and support public and private efforts to identify, evaluate, and protect historic and archeological resources. The National Register is under the auspices of the National Park Service. In New York State, the National and State Registers fall under the administration of the Office of Parks, Recreation, and Historic Preservation. Listed properties include: districts, sites, buildings, structures, and objects that are significant in American history, architecture, archeology, engineering and culture. Registered properties are distinguished by having been documented and evaluated according to uniform standards.

The necessity of this act was caused by ignorance and misunderstanding on many fronts in American society. The rapid expansion of the Interstate Highway System along with urban renewal programs in the late 1950s and early 1960s demolished established neighborhoods or so divided them that their sense of place was destroyed. Many historic buildings and properties were sacrificed in the name of progress. Regrettably, progress and preservation will always be at odds with each other.

Listed properties of Allegany County indicate the concern for historic preservation exhibited by residents. They include: location, name, and listing date.

ALFRED:
Terra Cotta Building—March 16, 1972

Steinheim Museum—June 4, 1973

Firemen's Hall—March 18, 1980

Alfred Village Historic District—September 11, 1985

Alumni Hall—September 12, 1985

ANGELICA:
Villa Belvidere Mansion—March 16, 1972

Old Allegany County Courthouse—August 21, 1972

Park Circle Historic District—January 31, 1978

Moses Van Campen House—April 16, 2004

BELFAST:
Rail and Titsworth Canal Warehouse—August 16, 2000

BELMONT:
Belmont Hotel—December 3, 2001

◄ *Belvidere Episcopal Church*

Belmont Library and Historical Society—July 5, 2003

BELVIDERE:
Christ Episcopal Church—May 17, 1974

BOLIVAR:
Bolivar Free Library—July 5, 2003

CANASERAGA:
Four Corners Historic District—March 6, 2002

CANEADEA:
Caneadea Bridge—November 19, 1998

CUBA:
South Street Historic District—May 26, 1988

Main Street Historic District—February 5, 1999

McKinney Stables—August 12, 1999

FRIENDSHIP:
Wellman House—June 20, 1974

WELLSVILLE:
Erie Depot—August 27, 1987

U.S. Post Office—May 11, 1989

WEST ALMOND:
West Almond Churches—August 2, 2002

New York State Historic Markers

This program was conceived in 1923 as a direct result of the soon to be celebrated 150th Anniversary of the American Revolution. The goal of the program was to mark specific locations of historic significance in local areas. Over the next few decades, the New York State Education Department placed signs of two sizes: the small ones denoted a historic place or event in that immediate locale while the larger ones explained the history of that area.

The small signs remaining today are listed as to locale:

ANGELICA: Sign in front of the Until the Day Dawns Cemetery honoring Angelica Pioneers.

BURNS: Signs mark locations of first resident and first schoolhouse in Canaseraga.

CANEADEA: Sign on Route 19 in Houghton explaining Jockey Street.

SCIO: Sign on Bill Allen Hill Road explaining first successful oil well in New York State: Triangle No. 1.

WELLSVILLE: Sign on Route 417 East denoting first fish survey in New York State.

Large signs are located in:

BOLIVAR: Sign at the Pioneer Oil Museum explaining "This Is Oil Country."

FRIENDSHIP: Sign in the rest area on I-86 eastbound lane between Friendship and Belvidere, describing the history of the Genesee Valley.

Local Historical Societies and Collections

County-owned collections and records are housed in Belmont and include:

COUNTY COURTHOUSE: County Clerk's Office holdings include Federal and New York State Census records, legal documents including land transaction, court records, marriage records from 1905 to 1935, early maps and many miscellaneous records.

COUNTY HISTORIAN'S OFFICE AND COUNTY MUSEUM: Holding extensive collection of local historical records and genealogical materials.

SURROGATE'S COURT: Holds wills, probates, and related legal materials.

A town list of historical societies and holdings includes the following:

ALFRED: Alfred Historical Society—collection housed in Alfred State College Library.

Alfred State College Archives—named the Jean Lang Western New York Historical Collection, is housed in college library.

Alfred University Archives—housed in Herrick Memorial Library.

ALMOND: Historical Society—holdings in their museum, the Hagadorn House.

AMITY: Allegany County Historical Society—no holdings.

Allegany County Museum—county collection housed in museum.

ANDOVER: Andover Historical Society—holdings in Town Hall.

BELFAST: Belfast Historical Society—holdings in their museum building, which was donated by Paul and Marion Fleming and Eugene and Peggy Watts.

BOLIVAR: Bolivar, Richburg, Alma, and Genesee, BRAG Historical Society—holdings in Bolivar Public Library.

Pioneer Oil Museum.

CANEADEA: Town holdings—in Town Hall.

CUBA: Cuba Cheese Museum, the newest museum in Allegany County held a preview opening on November 27, 2004.

Cuba Historical Society—holdings in their museum.

FRIENDSHIP: Friendship-Nile Historical Society.

HUME: Fillmore History Club.

Hume Town Museum—collection housed in the first town-owned museum in the county.

RUSHFORD: Rushford Historical Society—holdings in their museum.

WELLSVILLE: Mather Homestead—holdings in its museum.

Thelma Rogers Genealogical and Historical Society—holdings in their Dyke Street Museum.

Top: Pioneer Oil Museum in Bolivar

Bottom: Moss Lake, Town of Caneadea

Old Mill at Wiscoy Falls

WILLING: Willing Historical Society—no holdings but meets monthly in Town Hall.

WIRT: Richburg-Wirt Historical Society—holdings in their museum.

Places of Historical Significance

Allegany County has many natural resources that possess scenic and historic value. Among them are:

FORBIDDEN TRAIL SIGN: Located just east of Andover marking an Indian trail whose use was forbidden to the white pioneers.

MOSS LAKE: Located on Sand Hill Road in Caneadea, Moss Lake is a Registered Natural Landmark with the U.S. Department of the Interior that was formed by retreating glaciers and subsequent peat mining. It is home to rare plants.

SENECA COUNCIL HOUSE MARKER: The Catherine Schuyler Chapter of the Daughters of the American Revolution (DAR) placed a large boulder with an inscribed bronze plaque denoting the site where Moses Van Campen ran the gantlet in 1782. Located here was the famous Seneca Council House that was moved to present-day Letchworth State Park in 1871–72. This marker can be seen on the Council House Road in the Town of Caneadea.

SENECA OIL SPRING RESERVATION: Located near Cuba Lake, this is the oldest known oil discovery in North America. It was mapped by French missionaries in 1627.

WISCOY FALLS: Located in the Town of Hume on County Road 27 are three very scenic waterfalls. Upstream from the falls, Rochester Gas and Electric constructed a dam to provide water power for generating electricity.

Wiscoy Falls, Town of Hume

OTHERS: There are also many historic properties located throughout Allegany County that are privately owned and respect must be accorded when viewing them. Some of these properties are: Governor Higgins House in Rushford, the Hatch House in Friendship, the Mill at Wiscoy Falls, the Octagon House in Genesee, the Pink House in Wellsville, PS&N holdings on the County Fairgrounds, the Van Wickle House in Angelica, and the Willetts Estate in Belmont.

chapter 16

OUR COUNTY GOVERNMENT

Allegany County became a legal entity on April 7, 1806, and the entire county government probably consisted of no more than six people. The population was no more than four hundred people. Today, the population is about fifty thousand with about four hundred working for the county government. The county's unofficial "founder" was Philip Church who became the first judge. He named his settlement "Angelica" after his mother, Angelica Schuyler Church. In the middle of the Park Circle, Church placed a marker designating the center of the township.

The county seat remained in Angelica until 1859 when the Board of Supervisors voted to relocate to Belmont due to the fact the Erie Railroad, which opened in 1851, came through Belmont and not Angelica. Access to county offices in Belmont was now much easier and faster. When the move was first proposed, the people of Angelica vehemently objected. To assuage their sentiments, the New York State Legislature voted to hold court in both places, essentially creating a "two-shire county" until the mid-1890s, when court was held only in Belmont. The County Department of Social Services remained in Angelica at the old County Home site until moving to Belmont in 1976. (See Chapter 5 for additional information.)

County Home, Infirmary, and Farm

One of the most interesting yet saddest chapters of the county's rich history involves the old County Home in Angelica. When the need arose, the County Board of Supervisors authorized the construction of an Alms House in the 1830s. It was located two miles east of Angelica on present-day County Road 2. It housed many homeless, indigents, needy children, and senior citizens in need of medical attention and some with mental disabilities. The 180-acre farm was nearly self-sufficient as they raised, grew, or produced almost everything they needed.

There were two fires of significance: the first occurred in February of 1918 when the men's dormitory burned to the ground. All thirty-eight residents escaped safely. The second fire occurred in March of

◄ *County Home Buildings in Angelica, circa 1910*

This page: County Home Administration Building Fire, 1923

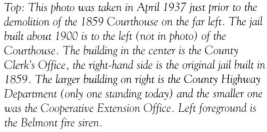

Top: This photo was taken in April 1937 just prior to the demolition of the 1859 Courthouse on the far left. The jail built about 1900 is to the left (not in photo) of the Courthouse. The building in the center is the County Clerk's Office, the right-hand side is the original jail built in 1859. The larger building on right is the County Highway Department (only one standing today) and the smaller one was the Cooperative Extension Office. Left foreground is the Belmont fire siren.

Middle: This County Jail, built about 1900, was torn down in 1976. The new County Office Building was built on this site in 1975–1976.

Bottom: Tearing down the old jail in October 1976.

1923 when the Administration Building, dining hall, women's dormitory, kitchen, and boiler room were destroyed. Tragically, nine residents lost their lives and nearly all records were destroyed. The men's dormitory, having been rebuilt after the fire in 1918, was saved only by tearing down a connecting corridor. The Angelica firemen were greatly hampered in their effort because the threads on the hydrants on the grounds did not match those of their equipment. (See Oramel Fire of 1937 in Chapter 12.)

The Allegany County Department of Social Services, as it is known today, began at roughly the time the County Alms House started. This department has grown in proportion to the needs of the county's residents. In February of 1975, the County Health Department was organized and based in the old County

Top: Steel erection crew for new County Office Building, 1975. Front row, left to right, are Clayton "Rabbit" Gifford, foreman; Dick Halstrom, engineer; and George Heron, foreman. Back row, left to right, are Roland Jimerson, job steward; Tyler Heron, connector; Arthur Schinder, welder; Paul Lee, ironworker; and Virgil Seneca, connector. Many workers were from Buffalo Iron Workers Local No. 6 and came from the Seneca Reservations at Cattaraugus and Allegany.

Middle: Completing the steel framework on the County Office Building. The flag attached to the steel beam was donated by Belmont American Legion Post No. 808.

Bottom: The new County Office Building was dedicated on November 19, 1976. Legislators present, left to right, are Robert McNinch, Leonard Warson, Harlan Hale, John Hasper, Richard Shelley, James Raptis, Donald King, and Max Freeman. (Photo courtesy of Olean Times-Herald)

189

Home as well. When the new County Office Building in Belmont opened in November of 1976, these two departments along with the Office of the County Historian relocated to Belmont. This marked the end of any county department based in Angelica, the site of the first county seat.

Shortly after these departments relocated to Belmont, the county sold the remaining Angelica buildings and land, but retained ownership and responsibility for about two acres comprising the cemetery. This cemetery started shortly after the Alms House opened around 1830, obviously out of necessity. Tragically, all graves are unnamed except one. The unmarked graves were designated by small marble tombstones and inscribed with only a number. Records matching names with burial numbers were lost in the Fire of 1923. Subsequently, the numbered stones were arranged to form two large monuments. Today, the entire cemetery is beautifully maintained by the County Department of Public Works.

The only named grave is that of Joe Henry Thomas who died on May 16, 1961, at the age of 113. Joe Henry was a teenager during the Civil War and a former slave. He was reportedly the son of a Jacksonville, Florida slave family that had once lived in Birdsall and worked on various Allegany County farms. He was very well known and liked throughout the Angelica community. Every Sunday, Ed Fleming or William Heaney Sr. would bring Joe Henry to Mass at Sacred Heart Roman Catholic Church in Angelica. Joe Henry's grave is in the northwest corner of the cemetery under a large pine tree.

Top: At the first meeting of the County Legislature in the new building, November 1976, are (left to right on the dais) Clerk of the Board Frances Barnes, Chairman Harlan Hale, and County Attorney James Sikaris. (Photo courtesy of Olean Times-Herald)

Bottom: Supreme, County, and Family Court Judge William Serra swearing in new County Clerk Joseph Presutti and County and Supreme Court Clerk Sally Young in January 1976.

"Buildings High on the Hill"

COURTHOUSE: In 1859, the first of the new county seat buildings was constructed on "Table Knoll," the highest point in the Village of Belmont. The present Allegany County Courthouse was constructed in 1937, replacing the original building of 1859. It was dedicated on July 20, 1938. On this date, the Board of Supervisors met there for the first time in the room currently called the Family Courtroom. For decades prior to 1938, the Board met in the Belmont Hotel, as this was the only place large enough to accommodate the twenty-nine-member Board, staff, press, and spectators. In the new Courthouse, the Supervisors Chamber then included the present chambers of Judge James E. Euken. When the current County Office Building, connected to the Courthouse, opened in 1976, the Board of Legislators had their own chamber and the former supervisors chamber was partitioned creating the Family Courtroom and chambers for the senior judge.

In 1806, the county consisted of only one town, Angelica. In 1808 it was "sub-divided," making a total of five towns. As the population grew along with people's associated needs, more towns were created. The last town formed was Ward in 1857 with lands taken from Alfred and Amity, making a total of twenty-nine. Each town supervisor represented his or her town on the County Board of Supervisors with a "weighted voting" system based on population. This system eventually proved cumbersome and in 1969 the Board voted to change to a Board of Legislators effective January 1, 1970. A person could run for either town supervisor or county legislator. The county was divided into five legislative districts with three legislators per district with equal voting power. Additionally, no one town could have more than one legislator. This caveat was later dropped. Individual district's population by law must be equal or within 5 percent of each other. Today, there are about ten thousand people per district. Population shifts based on the latest federal census data cause district lines to be redrawn periodically.

COUNTY OFFICE BUILDING: The Flood of 1972 wrought havoc throughout the County. (See Chapter 13.) The federal aid to the county contributed heavily to economic recovery. Through frugal management of this money on the part of county legislators, funding for a new County Office Building was now possible. After the idea was made public, critics questioned the need for this "huge" building,

Top left: Deputy Sheriff Jim Richardson on duty in the ground floor control room in 1976. Sheriff Reynard Meacham instituted wearing of uniforms about 1979.

Top right: Deputy Sheriff Jim Richardson on duty in the same place in May 2005. Security cameras in the building are attached to his monitor screen and his typewriter has been replaced by a computer.

Bottom left: Retired Sheriff Vanama Jones was killed in a car accident on August 12, 1969.

Bottom right: Mrs. Vanama Jones served as the jail matron.

saying it was not needed, it cost too much and they saw no need for the excessive number of proposed jail cells. After extensive and sometimes controversial debates, the County Legislature voted on June 24, 1974, in favor of building a new County Office Building. Legislator Leonard Watson of West Almond served as chairman of the Special Building Project Committee. Ribbon-cutting and dedication ceremonies took place on Friday afternoon at 1 p.m., November 19, 1976, as Board Chairman Harland Hale presided. Immediate benefits were realized when major county departments were now under one roof and the jail met new state criteria.

NEW COUNTY JAIL: Allegany County would soon prove the cliché correct that "History Repeats Itself." By the mid-1990s, overcrowding in the jail became common. New state mandates regarding housing of inmates dictated the county must build a new jail facility. The problem is compounded by the fact that the inmate population sometimes exceeds the number of available cells, necessitating the "boarding-out" of inmates to other county jails. This is done at great financial burden on our county.

As a result, the County Legislature voted on Monday, September 8, 2003, to build a new jail facility on a county-owned fifty-seven-acre plot south of Belmont on Route 19. As of April 2005, Sheriff Randal Belmont indicated the new jail could be in use by summer, 2006.

NEW COUNTY COURTHOUSE: In December 2004, the New York State Unified Court System Capital Review Board warned the County Legislature that the court facilities have not complied with the board's facility requirements for a state record of seventeen years. The Review Board has told the county to devise a plan of compliance.

Above: County Board of Legislators and County Staff, January 2005. Left to right, front row, are Edgar Sherman, Brent Reynolds, Rodney Bennett, and Sue Myers. Middle row: Patrick Regan, William Dibble, Chairman James Palmer, Curtis Crandall, Kenneth Nielsen, and Edmund Burdick. Top row: James Graffrath, Deputy Clerk Adele Finnemore, Clerk Brenda Rigby Riehle, Robert Sobeck, Daniel Russo, Ronald Truax, Robert Heineman, County Administrator John Margeson, and County Attorney Daniel J. Guiney.

Left: Aerial view of new jail, Route 19, south of Belmont, May 2005. (Photo courtesy of Sheriff Randal Belmont)